My Story

By Nurse Myra Bennett
The Florence Nightingale of the North

DRC PUBLISHING

3 Parliament Street
St. John's, Newfoundland and Labrador
A1A 2Y6
Telephone: (709) 726-0960
E-mail: staceypj@nl.rogers.com
www.drcpublishingnl.com

© **Myra Bennett, 2012**

Library and Archives Canada Cataloguing in Publication

Bennett, Myra
      My story / Myra Bennett.

ISBN 978-1-926689-47-0

      1. Bennett, Myra. 2. Nurses--Newfoundland and

Labrador--Biography. I. Title.

RT37.B46A3 2012   610.73092   C2012-902011-7

Layout and design by Becky Pendergast
Photographs on cover and in book courtesy of Trevor Bennett

Published 2012
Printed in Canada

We acknowledge the financial support of the Government of Canada through
the Canada Book Fund (CBF) for our publishing activities.

We acknowledge the financial support of the Government of Newfoundland and
Labrador through the Department of Recreation, Tourism and Culture for our
publishing activities.

Foreword

By Trevor Bennett

I was born in 1926 and started school one day short of my fourth birthday. My parents were very busy people. In later years I joked with my mother about putting me in school so young. We always had an extremely good maid and I wondered if Mom had put me in school early as a babysitting service.

My mother, Myra (Grimsley) Bennett, was the district nurse, stationed in our home community of Daniel's Harbour on the Northern Peninsula. She arrived from England in 1921, the same year she began a long career of caring for people along 200 miles of isolated rugged coast.

Mom was a wife and mother as well as a busy nurse, at the same time my father, Angus Bennett, was working tirelessly to make a living, build a home, support a wife and make her work his priority in everything he did. Her task would have been impossible without the man she married. He made a living from the sea and land and from the sweat of his brow. He put food on the table for everyone who came his way. He built a barn to house his horse, cow and chickens. In the barn was a spare stall for a visitor's horse. He made a shed to store preserved barrels of herring, seal meat and dry capelin to feed dog teams coming through from St Anthony. People who wanted to get to Deer Lake to connect with the train and go on to St John's had to travel the ten-day, two-week trail by dog team. The lifestyle of people who lived from the 1920 into the 2000's has been such a revolution of change, it is almost impossible to imagine today.

This book is a memoir my mother, Nurse Myra Bennett, wrote in the 1960's. My mother was not only a wife and mother and nurse, she was a shoulder to cry on in times of sorrow. She was a shelter in a storm, she was an educator, she was the lady with the lantern and, most of all, she was a warm and loving human being. She was a person who was very anxious to serve her people, in doing so she was serving her God. My mother never wore her religion on her sleeve, but she was a deeply religious person who would attend and join in singing and prayer in any church.

She felt she had a duty to all the children of God, age, colour, creed; status had no bearing on her duty. Being stationed at Daniel's Harbour made it impossible for her to get a patient out from her care once the coastal boat stopped its run in December until May. I remember with amazement her agility in going up the stairs in our home, two steps at a time, with a lighted lamp in one hand (there was no electricity) and a plate in the other. I remember the perpetual tooth extractions at our kitchen table, many times with someone holding a flashlight directed so Mom could see which tooth to take out. She would never let a person suffer toothache through the night, she was always aware she might be called away on another medical emergency before daylight. I shall never forget the morning she came home grief stricken. She had lost her first mother after 700 successful deliveries. She was devastated, her world had suddenly crashed.

As her story unfolds, I am sure readers may wonder how such conditions and times could ever have existed during the period of our history in which she lived, worked and loved. As Dr.Noel Murphy once said, "There will never be another Nurse Bennett and hopefully there will never be such need."

Table of Contents

	Page	
Chapter One	1	England
Chapter Two	27	The Decision to go Overseas
Chapter Three	30	Newfoundland
Chapter Four	36	Daniel's Harbour
Chapter Five	43	My District
Chapter Six	47	A Visit from the Governor, Work, Love and Marriage
Chapter Seven	54	Life in Newfoundland
Chapter Eight	62	My Kitchen Cases
Chapter Nine	76	Early Years
Chapter Ten	84	The Baby in the Barn
Chapter Eleven	87	Fried Rabbit, Halibut and Stew
Chapter Twelve	92	Appendix Trouble
Chapter Thirteen	94	Winter
Chapter Fourteen	100	Hallelujah!
Chapter Fifteen	106	Training Midwives
Chapter Sixteen	111	A Man of Vision
Chapter Seventeen	116	A Visit to England
Chapter Eighteen	129	Community Work
Chapter Nineteen	133	Merry Christmas
Chapter Twenty	136	TB a Challenge but not all Work
Chapter Twenty-one	139	Diary Excerpts 1940s
Chapter Twenty-two	141	The Life of a Working Mother
Epilogue	145	

Myra as a district nurse in England

Preface

I have so often been asked to write something of my experiences in my years of nursing service, both in Newfoundland and elsewhere, and I wonder always where does one start on a resume of one's life that would be interesting to read? My conclusion is that the only place to start is at the beginning.

I was born Myra Maud Grimsley in London, England on April 1, 1890. My parents were Stephen Alexander Grimsley and Patti Ellen (Crapper) Grimsley.

My mother, in fact, was the sister of Thomas Crapper, who is credited with inventing the modern day flush toilet. He invented the Silent Valveless Water Waste Preventer, a ball and suction device which allows an efficient flush with a minimum amount of water and also shuts off the flow to the tank. In 1880, his company, Thomas Crapper Co. Ltd, was so well known that he was invited to supply plumbing to Sandringham House, home of Edward VII, the Prince of Wales, and to other Royal notables. He also supplied the drainage for Westminister Abbey. There is a memorial stone for him in Westminister Abbey. He was honoured with a knighthood for his contributions and hard work. He died January 27, 1910.

I was one of seven children in a working class family, I left school at age 14 and worked in a tailor shop for six years before training as a nurse at Woolwich and completing a midwifery course at Clapham School of Midwifery. I worked as a nurse in England for ten years, from 1911 to 1921, before I was persuaded to come to Newfoundland by Lady Harris, wife of Sir Charles Alexander Harris, the then Governor of Newfoundland.

On September 13, 1920, I signed a contract with the Newfoundland Outport Nursing Association (NONA) agreeing to work as a district nurse in Newfoundland for a period of two years from the date of my arrival at a salary of $1,000 a year. I also agreed to undertake the work of a midwife without the assistance of a doctor.

In May of 1921, I arrived in Daniel's Harbour, a tiny community on Newfoundland's Northern Peninsula, and was surprised to learn that I was the first district nurse ever known in that area.

In January of 1922 I married Angus Bennett, a fisherman and ex-merchant marine. Angus and I settled in the house he built and it was there we raised a family of three children, two daughters and a son. I was a wife and mother, and I was also a working nurse whose career spanned more than 50 years. During that time, I delivered more than 700 babies and extracted at least 5,000 teeth. My long career of caring for people along 200 miles of isolated coast began and ended in Daniel's Harbour.

Chapter One

England

As one gets older, one's thoughts go back to the childhood days, its hopes and fears, its disappointments and rewards. Among my earliest memories is of a Christmas day in London when the table was ready for the family to sit and eat. A child came to the door asking my mother to go to see her mother who was ill. Leaving the dinner, my mother accompanied the child to her house, but returned quite soon, bringing with her several other children, and proceeding to sit them down to the dinner which we were waiting to eat. I was told to go and help at the house from which the children had been brought, and upon reaching there had to light a fire. It was very cold and I thought wistfully of our warm home and the dinner I was so badly wanting.

My elder brother was also roped in; he had to make kindling for me. My mother was in an adjoining room with the sick woman. The family was desperately poor – no fuel – no food – and the mother, though I did not know it then, was about to give birth. My mother was not trained but apparently knew enough to see the poor woman safely through her ordeal, and I was delighted to see a brand new baby, and to hold it after it was washed. Then of course, some dinner had to be provided for the woman, so again, my brother and I carried food and drink, as well as coal, to the house. My brother and I looked ruefully at the remains of the dinner when we had a chance to eat, but I shall never forget the faces of those children to whom a decent meal was a novelty, and I felt so proud of my mother who could go into a strange home and bring peace out of chaos.

Not that I did not resent having to give up my dinner and spend my Christmas day doing a dirty job of fire lighting, especially as we had our new clothes on, but we decided it was worth it to see the family fed, the new baby warm and cared for, and the father's gratitude when he came home from a futile search for help to find things all smoothed out. These acts of charity were part of my mother's creed. I have wakened sometimes to find a naked child being put into my bed. The family had been evicted. They were sitting in the street with their belongings when my mother insisted on collecting the children, bringing them home, giving them a bath, and putting them in our beds after being sure they were not verminous.

Thus my training in helping those less fortunate began in my early childhood. It used to be a great wonder to me to know my mother could go into a home – and then there was a new baby there. She taught me how to make baby shirts and usually there was one around when needed. Then the time came when I had to get out to work for my living. At age 13, I had been ahead at the higher grade school I attended but I could not leave until the legal age of 14 so, of course, before my birthday, arrangements were made for me to start work with a German tailor.

A couple of days after my fourteenth birthday, I was sitting in the workroom of my employer from 8 a.m. until 1 p.m. An hour was taken for dinner, then back to the chair from 2 p.m. till 8 p.m. although half an hour was supposed to be taken for tea. For this 10-1/2 hour workday, five days a week, plus the shorter Saturday of 7-1/2 hours, I received the sum of six shillings. To reach the place of business in time, I had to rise at 6 a.m. and walk across London which took just over an hour, and at night another hour to get home. I preferred walking to taking the bus because after sitting all day I was glad to stretch my legs a bit.

I spent most evenings at the Hoxton Market Christian Mission, taking Bible classes and taking part in Gospel services as well as teaching sewing for an hour. These 'classes' were held at the Mission headquarters in the slum district of Hoxton. Among the activities with which I helped was the meeting held for the derelict men and women whose only 'home' consisted of a park bench at night, and walking about all day seeking a meal or a job of some kind which would produce a few coppers with which to buy a meal.

Members of the Mission would go looking for these poor people and bring them to the Mission where they were given hot cocoa, bread and jam, and a wash. Various garments were available, having been collected from more or less well-to-do people, but of course many of these garments were in need of repair and alteration. That's where I was able to help; I could sew.

In a separate room, a man would be invited to choose an outfit as good a fit as could be found and after he had donned it I would size things up and see what alterations, if any, were needed. The man would then resume his original rags while I tackled the newer garments, maybe shortening pants or sleeves or attaching a necessary patch. Meanwhile, a Gospel service was being held in the large hall where hymn singing seemed to add to the comfort of the poor derelicts. Of course, the usual story of drunkenness as well as other misfortunes were told. But there was a great deal of heroism evidenced when one of the crowd tried to return to a former well conducted life.

I remember an occasion when I had a man awaiting the result of my work on a garment who asked if he could try to play the organ. He was led to the seat and I shall never forget the music that came forth. He had been the organist at a large fashionable church but had succumbed to drink, lost his employment, then became unacceptable at the church and had deteriorated to such an extent that the Thames embankment benches were the only home he had.

How he played – his very soul seemed to pour forth – and we did not disturb him. After a while he stopped. He gathered up the mended garments I had for him and was about to leave. As I was leaving at the same time he offered to accompany me and when we reached my home he agreed to come in for a cup of tea.

He subsequently became a regular visitor and gave me my first music lesson. Happily he succeeded in staying away from alcohol and got a decent job. One wonders how many of these broken lives were mended by the activities of the Hoxton Market Christian Mission, which owed its existence to the work of two brothers, Lewis and John Burtt, who founded it in 1881 and literally gave their lives for those less fortunate.

So life proceeded for me – early to rise – a full day's work – then the Mission at night. Tailoring then was of course a seasonal job and as I worked for tailors who in turn made the clothes for a famous Savile Row firm the seasons were governed by various things, like the court sessions when famous people were received by the reigning monarch. There would be the usual rush for dress suits for a levee – for yachting clothes during that season or motor coats for the new horseless carriages which were just becoming used.

So many unpronounceable names of European notabilities who came to be dressed as well as the American millionaires who would order as many as 40 complete outfits at a time. I became more expert at my job so my income started to rise and eventually I reached the magnificent salary of 30 shillings per week. I could go no higher and was not content to work as I was doing with no opportunity of advancement.

Then it was, in discussing matters with the Mission superintendent that the suggestion was made that I consider nurses' training. With much trepidation I agreed to apply for probationer's training, and to my surprise I was accepted.

The years that followed are somewhat hazy now, but I remember long hard days of work in a small hospital where I was often too tired to sleep, where there always seemed to be an emergency, where I knew nobody outside the hospital and would cheerfully have returned to my former job. However, the turning point came when I overheard someone at the outpatients' door being told that the person in the ambulance could not be admitted because it was not a maternity hospital and there was no midwife on the staff. In my ignorance I thought it did not matter about having a midwife – a hospital was the place where sick people were looked after under any and all conditions. After hearing that I decided I would become a midwife when I was free from general training.

Because I wanted to nurse the poorest people I joined a district nursing home, where nurses were trained in the homes of the patients. There, I qualified as a maternity nurse but found that I was still not qualified to attend the delivery of babies by myself. In my ignorance I had considered a maternity nurse and a midwife to be one and the same. I knew now what I needed was the coveted Central Midwives Board Certificate.

In the meantime, World War One had commenced and as many of the doctors had been called up for active service, I was often left with difficult cases for which I was not trained, nor qualified. Then I had a chance to train at the British Hospital for Mothers and Babies in Woolwich, London, and because I could not afford to pay for this training, I signed an agreement to serve as district midwife for three years after graduation. So in June 1915, I took up residence in Woolwich and had the happiest and busiest, as well as the most terrifying, six months of my life.

Zepplin raids were being carried out by the Germans and of course the arsenal at Woolwich was a prime target. Total blackouts were the order of the day, and it was difficult to find one's way to homes where babies were about to arrive. The hospital was filled to capacity with patients and babies, and during raids we had to carry both mothers and babies down to the basement in case of a hit or flying debris.

There were no reinforced air raid shelters in those days – it was an entirely new concept of warfare. Patients who had heart trouble were of course not moved but stayed in a small ward where I was ordered to stay with them. It was considered that I was able to not only keep calm but was not really scared. I must have been a good actress because I was really frightened. However we were lucky enough that we did not get a direct hit and in the daylight the patients were all returned to their beds.

The British Hospital for Mothers and Babies had instituted a course of training lasting six month for nurses who had already taken their general training and a year for all others in 1905. I received my certificate allowing me to practise as a midwife on December 20, 1915, having passed the examination of the Central Midwives Board. I then returned to Woking, a town in northwest Surrey, about 25 miles from London, to fulfill my obligation for the next three years.

How thankful I was that I had the tuition under the founders of the Woolwich hospital. These three women, Mrs. Lelia Parnell, Miss Alice Gregory, who was an acquaintance of Florence Nightingale, and Miss Maud Cashmore gave their lives to found and carry on the training of the higher class of midwife. They gave a small silver acorn to every graduate which bears the motto, "Esto sol testis" (Let the sun be my witness), and we were taught to live up to those words. How often we heard the Matron and her assistants tell us "Let your lives be so honest, your work so excellent that no strongest rays of the sun can reveal a fault."

War conditions were as rigid in Surrey as in London. Woking was an important junction on the railway to Portsmouth on the south coast and a port for ships crossing the Channel with troops and materials. The district where I worked had seen many changes since the start of war. Woking was a nice quiet country town when I took up the post of district nurse and midwife but the outbreak of war changed all that. Factories opened, aeroplane works and various other works came into the neighbourhood, an army pay corps was stationed near the town, refugees arrived from London, and the railway junction was one of the important ones through which supplies passed en route to France.

We became used to the roar of planes being tested over our roof tops before they were sent to the war areas. The constant rumble of trains, the blackout, the scarcity of food, the arrival of refugees from London, the increasing number of births to attend, and, alas, the dwindling number of doctors and nurses to help, as one after another was called into the war effort made this period an unforgettable one. Looking back, one wonders how one survived fit and able to continue.

District nursing was harder than ever during the next three years. The population of the district had increased as a result of war but the number of doctors had greatly decreased. Of the 24 doctors previously in the district, only two elderly doctors had been left to carry out duties during the war. The other doctors were busy with the army, and only one or two other midwives were available as many other nurses had joined the forces.

The scarcity of doctors meant that I had to do things that I would never have been allowed to do if doctors had been available. The Central Midwives Board had a set of rules under which certain conditions called for the presence of a doctor, whether the midwife could deal with it or not. Consequently it was necessary to fill in the usual form in triplicate to summon help as the occasion arose. Having done this, the nurse carries on to the best of her ability.

During these war years it was usual, when I summoned the doctor, that he would arrive almost too tired to help and ask me to apply the forceps while he gave the anesthetic. Naturally, I was glad to have to do this and to know the doctor had enough faith in me to permit me to do it. This experience became of great value when I started to work in Newfoundland. Then again I built up a reputation for not sending for the doctor unless the condition was absolutely necessary, so I was assured of a quick response when I did ask for a doctor's help.

The Home from which I worked was on the crest of a hill and it was an easy matter to freewheel on my bicycle down the long hill until one reached the right-angle turn on the highroad. At this turn, a railway bridge crossed the road overhead. So I always slowed down on approaching the turn because it was impossible to see if any traffic would be approaching from round the corner.

Complete blackout was the order of the day, or should I say night? To comply with blackout regulations, I had darkened my bicycle light by pasting tissue paper over the glass and directed the light downward so that it would not be seen above. One dark night a phone call summoned me to a baby case so I set forth, whizzing down the hill, only slowing when I heard a loud voice say "Stop!"

I thought it was someone playing games so I did not stop. A few yards ahead another voice said "Stop," so I slowed down and to my surprise found myself looking at the business end of a bayonet. Had I proceeded even at the slow rate I was going then I would have had an accident because the space under the bridge had been filled with vehicles to stop anyone from going through.

The soldier who stopped me explained the roadblock was because of possible saboteurs and then asked me for identification: where I was going and why. I explained that I was in a hurry to see an expectant mother but he would not accept my word. Luckily, a man standing by identified me as the district nurse and vouched for me whereon I was permitted to go on after the soldier had removed enough of the barrier to get my bicycle through. I learned afterwards that there had been rumours that lights were being used to guide air attacks to the railway junction.

There were funny incidents during the war years too, as when I was asked by a small girl to bring her mother a baby. Her father had been on active service for a long time, but I promised I would see her father when he was home and ask him if he would like me to bring a boy or a girl. A few days later, a nearby neighbour of the child had twins and when I visited the patient next morning to attend to mother and babies, the child rushed at me like a young tornado, saying: "You are a liar – you said you had no babies, and you go and give that woman two babies, and you would not give me one."

A sadder experience was that of a young Belgium refugee who had a stillborn baby. The woman had suffered so much during the evacuation and could speak no English, but believed that her baby could not die because her priest had given her a bottle of holy water from her church in Belgium. She believed the water would bring the child back to life. Her despair was dreadful. Her husband was on active service and this was her first baby. Here she was among strangers who did not speak her language, although they were kind to her.

What tragedies were caused as the result of war. I can remember the anxiety among our neighbours during the earlier Boer War, when so many husbands and sons had gone to Africa, and the jubilation when news of the relief of Mafeking was announced. As I had no immediate relatives involved in that war it meant little or nothing to me personally, but my time was now coming in the world's greater war.

The busy years at Woking seemed endless, with the worry of brothers in the firing line, my parents in London undergoing Zeppelin raids, the scarcity of food and the shortages of medical help. At the Home from which I worked there was no other certified midwife on the staff and there was too much general nursing to be done to permit me to do only midwifery, so the need for extra care, not to cross-infect, kept me on my toes.

There were some terminal cancers needing daily care and one of these was a man who picked me an apple each day from the tree in his garden. Unfortunately, he insisted on keeping it under his pillow and just as I had finished with him and was ready to leave, he would produce it saying, "Tis a Coxes Orange Pippin, Nurse. I knew the man who raised them." I could only accept the apple gracefully and take it away, eventually destroying it. If only I could have eaten it; I was always hungry for fruit.

On one of my rounds, I saw a notice saying that heavy workers could get two ounces of bacon by applying at the town hall. Of course I applied – but the clerk told me regretfully that district nurses had not been listed as heavy workers. Porters, railway workers, etc. could get the bacon – I had to go without.

My headquarters was in charge of a lady who was a trained nurse but had no midwifery training, and this fact led to misunderstanding and frustration. Patients were supposed to call in person at the Home and give the particulars to the Matron, who would presumably inform the midwife (I was the only midwife there) and thus set in motion the ante-natal visits needed to insure the successful conclusion of the delivery of a healthy child and a well recovered mother.

Because this Matron considered that such care was not really necessary she would fail to give me the address of the patient so that ante-natal visits did not get paid with the frequency required. Consequently, I ran into difficulties which could have been avoided. One such incident happened when a woman sent in a hurry for me. I had not heard of her existence before but upon arrival at her house found her undergoing severe ante-partum hemorrhage. She had told the Matron in her interview that she would probably not meet the normal nine month date because she had never carried a child for the whole time – and that she was a "Bleeder." Happily, a doctor was available and the child and its mother made a good but slow recovery.

On another occasion a patient called at the Home to book me but again I was not told of the visit. A few days later the woman again called at the Home, bringing with her a nightdress stained with meconium (the early bowel contents of the fetus). She told Matron something was coming and she didn't know what it was. The Matron was highly disgusted with the sight of the nightgown and told the woman to go home and not bring such disgusting things for her to see. Later, when I returned from my rounds, I was told to go and see the patient. I found her prostrate with a baby born as far as the neck, with the head still to be born. The baby, of course, was dead. With the head not delivered the child had inspired fluid and so drowned.

How many tragedies could have been averted if the Matron had only confessed her ignorance of midwifery and permitted those who did know to conduct the affair.

A particularly unhappy case was that of a woman whose husband was away on active service, and who lived alone in a village a few miles outside Woking. This was her first pregnancy and she was so very much larger than normal that I was uneasy. It was such an isolated home, no telephone, and the nearest neighbour a good ways away, too far to permit me to leave the patient and run for help. Again no ante-natal care.

However, I had to do the best I could and the labour proceeded slowly. To my horror, eventually the child was born without any back to its head. The condition is known as anencephalus. The rest of the child was perfect, a beautiful face but it ended just over the eyebrows, just behind the ears, nothing but an empty cavity. Fortunately the child was dead, and I so arranged it that the mother did not see the horror. This was one time when I was glad of superstition. The mother explained that several months previously she had gone to the well for a bucket of water and had seen a child fall in and only the top of its head was seen above the water when the body was recovered. She said that was why the top of her baby's head was missing. What else could one do but agree?

I suppose I was so unnerved by this experience, the blackness of the surroundings, and the overhanging trees under which I had to go along the lanes that when I mounted my bicycle to go home I thought a hand clutched me on my back. Thinking there might be a man prowling around looking for a victim, I rode as furiously as possible regardless of bumps or lights until I reached the Home where I hurried in and went to bed. Next morning in daylight, still nervous about the previous night's experience, I again went to get on my bike and had the same feeling of someone clutching at me, but there was nobody around. The cause, I finally discovered, was that my bicycle saddle had broken its spring and in getting on I had pushed up the saddle, thus giving me the feeling I mentioned. I was annoyed with myself for being so alarmed over nothing.

These incidents were not too worrying. It was the day-to-day nagging on the part of the Matron and the hiding away of what little food we could get that bothered me the most. Matron had a sister who lived in the north of England who used to send the occasional parcel of food, presumably for the staff. Needless to say, the staff never saw it and we were hugely pleased when one day Matron ran out of her bedroom with a swarm of wasps after her. Her sins had surely found her out. She had hidden several jars of jam in her room and presumably had opened some, enabling the wasps to find their way in. Of course they objected to having their feast interrupted and acted accordingly.

One very mean trick of hers was to take the ration of fresh milk, stand it away out of sight until the cream rose, skim the top for herself and let us have the skim. Another mean trick was to remove the pipe which ran from the gas stove to the main so that we could not get a hot drink when returning during the night from cases. I remember scrounging around one early morning before going to bed and finding only some custard powder, which I mixed with cold water and drank. Not too appetizing, but it stayed hunger pains.

When my three years passed and I told Matron I would be leaving in a month's time, she declared that was impossible, that cases were booked up, that she had no other nurse to take my place etc. So I stayed another month – still the same story – so I decided that come what may I would leave the very next month end.

By this time I had succeeded in getting a couple of rooms in which I had installed my parents and my youngest brother. My father had tried to enlist but he was overage and was sent to work in a munitions factory.

So I had a home of sorts in which to stay while I sorted out my thoughts and decided upon my next move. I was not home two days before I had a call from a patient who had expected to be nursed by a midwife from the Home I had just left but found nobody to attend her. The Matron had given her my address so of course I attended her but had to send the husband to ask for the bag of requirements which was the property of the Home. Upon completion of the case, I notified the Matron to send one of the nurses from the Home to complete the nursing period. After this happened several times, I found I was still doing work but with no salary and keeping myself on call. So once again I notified Matron that this case was the last one I would attend.

But now fate intervened.

In the fall of 1918 the Great War was winding down but then something erupted that seemed as harmless as the common cold. But the flu that season was far more than an ordinary cold.

In the two years it raged, the Spanish Flu killed 50 to 100 million people worldwide. It struck mainly those between 20 and 30. The Spanish Flu picked off so many who had become weakened during the privations of war. I delivered babies in beds occupied by other members of the family too prostrate to be moved.

It was inevitable that I should finally succumb to the flu and that was absolutely selfish of me, according to Matron, who 'nursed' me by opening the window and placing my bed under it, probably to avoid getting any infection from me. The most heartbreaking thing was to hear the doorbell and telephone conversations telling people that I was too sick to go to them.

Within a few weeks I had recovered enough to return to work. On November 11, 1918, I was called to a first-time pregnant woman about whom I had been so anxious that I had asked her to engage a doctor as well as me. She lived about four miles from me, her home being on a hill. I found I was too weak to ride all the way on my bicycle so I leaned on it going upgrades, rode on downgrades, and got there in due time. The doctor was much stronger than I was, but after giving the anesthetic he asked me to do the rest.

All went well, and after making the woman comfortable and seeing all was well with the baby and that the doctor could manage to get to his home again, I left for my headquarters. Having freewheeled down the hill, I had to walk the rest of the way, leaning on my bike.

I suddenly noticed that people were carrying bunting and small flags. One woman had a bulldog with a leash of tiny flags and I wondered what had happened for people to be doing such stupid things. Then a small boy whose mother

I had nursed not long before ran up to me and said, "Oh Nurse, isn't it wonderful?" "What is wonderful?" said I. "Why the war is over," said he.

The news was so unexpected, such an anti-climax, that momentarily I felt stunned. I just sat down on the curb and cried like a baby. Four years of agony, death, illness and starvation, all for what?

One brother dead in Gallipoli, one brother wounded and in hospital, one brother wounded enroute home with the probability of having a leg amputated, and another brother crossing the Atlantic on leave to Australia, from where he had volunteered. And a young brother who had been deprived of education because he had been evacuated from London because of air raids. All for what?

I had four brothers in uniform during World War One. Their ages were 14, 16, 18 and 20. My youngest brother, Sam, was only nine when the war started in 1914. My sister had died. My brother Steve was killed in Gallipoli, age 16. In his tunic pocket was a photograph of himself in uniform. A bullet had gone through the picture that was addressed to me in London and that I later received. My brothers Edward, Arthur and Will survived the war.

On the day the war ended, when I reached my headquarters and Matron saw my tear-stained face she asked me why I was crying. I stammered out that the war was over whereupon she laughed and said that was nothing to cry about. Of course it wasn't. But how could I explain to such an unsympathetic person about the heartaches of so many of my patients who had lost their loved ones and of the fatherless children who still hoped to see their fathers again.

So life gradually became more bearable, although some of the convalescing soldiers returning to their homes made one's heart ache. They were almost like strangers to their own children. Some of the men were incapacitated and wondered how they would be able to secure jobs and maintain their families.

My own brother, Edward, who had been in battle at age 14, was limping around on crutches, having had a compound fracture of the femur. When he was brought back from France he was put into a small hospital provided by Lady Astor, and in the room with him were three similarly wounded men.

It was decided that amputation was the only chance to save their lives, but my brother was obstinate and refused to have the operation performed. When told he would die otherwise he said,"Alright, but I will die with my leg on." The other three men did have their legs taken off, but unhappily they did not survive. It was almost a joke in the family that my brother was just too stubborn to die. For a while he walked with a calliper and crutches. But he eventually recovered and went on to become a trained engineer in aeroplane engines.

The war was finally over and the reconstruction of lives and homes and families had begun. The picking up of the threads, the healing of the wounded both physically and mentally, the closing of the gaps left by the deaths of our loved ones now became our goal. Gradually, food became less scarce, personnel were released from the services and returned to civilian life, doctors again became available, nurses came back to district work and the pressure upon some of us was eased.

Now that I had freed myself from the overwhelming unhappiness of working for the Association to which I had been tied for three years I was at a loss. But it was not long before I had offers of work from some of the doctors who had attended cases with me, and now asked me to do some private nursing.

It was during this period that a peculiar experience came my way. I was asked to nurse a man who had had an epileptic seizure and had fallen face down into the fireplace, which was still hot, although the fire had died down. As he had never had a seizure in his life, it was a great shock to him. He was an intelligent well educated man, comparatively well-to-do, with a responsible job. He was married with a wife and a small son. His face was badly burned and was very painful, especially as the mouth had been burned making feeding very difficult. The only food he could swallow with a little comfort was junket, which I used to keep ready for him all the time. His state of mind caused me more worry than his physical condition and as finances would not allow for another nurse, I had to do twenty-four hour duty. I found that reading in a very monotonous tone would sometimes get him to relax and fall asleep. So my evenings consisted of sitting by him after doing the dressings and murmuring nursery rhymes until he slept, when I would catch a nap myself. We discussed his job and, as he was so anxious, I suggested that he ask his employer to call and see him. He was horrified at the suggestion, saying it was impossible, that he himself would have to go to see his boss, who apparently was so important a personage that he could not be asked to do such a thing as call on an employee.

One night I dreamed that the patient (who was now able to get up and eat in the dining room) and I were just sitting over a final cup of tea when the doorbell rang. The maid, with the wife and child, had all gone to church, so of course I opened the door. I saw a man standing there, to whom I said, "Oh, you are Mr... (mentioning the name of my patient's boss). Won't you come in?" Opening the dining room door, I ushered him in and left them to their business.

Naturally I told the patient of this dream and he said that's not likely to happen. But strangely enough it did happen just as I dreamed it. Just the same conditions: a Sunday evening, the family away at church, the lingering over the cup of tea. The visitor wondered how I had known his name and my patient told him my dream. Eventually my patient was able to return to his job, and to the best of my knowledge did not have any recurrence of seizures.

A nurse friend recommended me for a holiday post in Wales, so I had a month or two there, relieving the district nurse who was able to take a holiday. But I still wished to be in the midwifery branch of nursing. So I went back to London to look for a job.

* * * *

That was when I accepted the post as midwife to the Rescue Home. In my district there was a Rescue Home run by the Church of England where unmarried girls were housed until labour commenced. This is when I was called to deliver the babies and to nurse the mother until she was able to return to her home, or to a situation after having made arrangements for the care of her baby.

The lady in charge was a dedicated person who had given her life to this work. During the time the girls were in her charge she gave them advice and comfort, arranged for spiritual consolation, and interviewed the acknowledged father to try to get him to assume responsibility for his child. A few marriages were the result of this help, and as well many girls were able to find situations where they were permitted to keep their child with them. Where this could not be arranged, Miss Todd would arrange for the fostering, with kindly women visiting the homes periodically to ensure that the babies had motherly care and love.

Miss Todd suggested that I take up residence at the Rescue Home as a staff midwife. A house was prepared for the patients, the upper rooms were fitted as small wards, and it was found much more convenient for all concerned because I could do ante-natal examination and keep a watchful eye on the girls without too much bother with visiting.

One expectant mother was my housemaid, coming in daily while still living in the house next door. After she had her baby another expectant mother would come to help me. Behind the house was a small chapel where daily prayers were said, with a visiting clergyman coming regularly for services. It was a beautiful little place, kept in spotless condition and frequently used by the girls when they had a spare moment to sit and mediate. Thus I was able to get to know the patients better than I had ever been able to with the rush of other district work.

So many sad stories I heard. So much despair, so many regrets. But they were brave and ready to shoulder responsibility when returned to society again. With all the girls who passed through my hands, I never had one who willingly gave up her baby. In some cases, where the girls' parents were not aware of their downfall, I have known the girls to take menial jobs so that if they could not keep the baby with them, they could support it in a home where they could visit it. In some cases these girls eventually married and took the child into the home provided by the husband, even if he were not the father, and we found these marriages quite successful. I lived with and nursed these girls for two years and they were the most peaceful two years I can remember. It was wonderful to have a superior who did not find fault with everything I did or did not do. The fact that food was easier to get, and of course I was responsible for the housekeeping costs, all helped to erase the misery of the previous three years from my mind.

Before assuming the job with the Rescue Home I had a visit from the chairman of the Home for which I had previously worked and was surprised to hear that the committee had asked him to request me to return and work with Matron. It appeared the nurses there had objected to Matron's behaviour and had left en masse so there was nobody to go to the patients who had been accepted. If I would go back in charge maybe the nurses would return. But the thought was so horrible I could not bring myself to consider it. I later heard the lady had been appointed as Matron to an inebriates' home. Still later I saw a picture of her in a nursing magazine. She was then a pupil midwife and I was glad to know she would learn some badly needed lessons.

Myra's brother Stephen was killed at Gallipoli during the First World War. A bullet went through the photograph of him which was in his tunic and addressed to Myra. The picture was picked up on the battlefield and sent to her.

Nurse Grimsley (back row) England, 1915

Alice Gregory (left) and Maud Cashmore were Myra's teachers at the British Hospital for Mothers and Babies

Myra Maud Grimsley with her parents and her younger brothers, Stephen and Sam

Stephen Alexander Grimsley, Myra's father, as a young man

Arthur Grimsley, Myra's brother, who served in the First World War and received a military medal and the Croix de Guerre

Myra and Nurse Harvey on ship crossing to Newfoundland in 1921

Patti Ellen (Crapper)
Grimsley, Myra's mother

Myra with bike she used
when going to cases in
England

Newfoundland Outport Nursing Association
'Agreement between Lady Harris - wife of
His Excellency The Governor of Newfoundland
and Nurse Myra M. Grimsley

The undersigned nurse - Myra M Grimsley
agrees to work as a District Nurse in Newfoundland
for a period of two years from the date of her
arrival in Newfoundland' at a salary of
1,000 dollars (one thousand dollars) a year.
The above mentioned nurse would also be prepared
to undertake the work of midwife without the
assistance of a doctor
                    Signature of nurse — Myra M Grimsley
                    Signature of Lady Harris — Constance Harris.

Signed & returned Sept 13ᵗʰ 1920

Copy of contract Myra signed in 1920

No.  Date Dec: 20th 1915.

Central Midwives Board.

(2 Edw. VII. ch. 17.)

We hereby Certify

That  *Myra Maud Grimsley*

having passed the Examination of the Central Midwives Board, and having otherwise complied with the rules and regulations laid down in pursuance of the Midwives Act, 1902, is entitled by law to practise as a Midwife in accordance with the provisions of the said Act and subject to the said rules and regulations.

F.H. Champneys.

Chapter 2

The decision to go overseas

It was while reading a nursing magazine that I came across an article telling of a woman who was in labour and whose husband had gone for a doctor some distance away. This was in a remote part of Canada and there were no near neighbours who could have stayed with the woman. When the husband returned, accompanied by the doctor, the intervening creek had risen so high with the pouring rain that they were unable to cross and had to wait until the water had lowered enough for them to cross. Upon reaching the home they found the mother and baby had died.

This seemed such a senseless waste of human life that I decided I would try to go to such places where women needed help. I applied to the Imperial Overseas Nursing Association (IONA) and was offered a post somewhere in Canada, as soon as passage could be arranged. At the time, all transatlantic transportation had been taken up by returning war personnel: Army, Navy, Air Force, together with wives and children. Shipping had been subjected to submarine and mine attacks, there was a dreadful shortage of passenger accommodation, and people wishing to travel just had to wait.

Both Lady Grey of Canada and Lady Harris of Newfoundland were concerned about conditions in isolated parts of Canada and Newfoundland, and Lady Grey had applied to the IONA for suitable women who would be willing and capable of grappling with these conditions. My name had been given to Lady Grey as a suitable qualified person but then the traveling problem arose.

These two ladies met in London and discussed the matter, whereupon Lady Harris suggested that, as the Furness Withy Line was sailing from Liverpool to St. John's, maybe a passage could be obtained more readily to Newfoundland than to Canada. She asked Lady Grey if she would relinquish my appointment to Canada, and asked me if I would agree to go to Newfoundland as one of the first nurses in the employ of the Newfoundland Outport Nursing Association (NONA). A meeting between us was arranged and I agreed to the change. Considering that the need for my services in Newfoundland was as great as the need on the Canadian prairies, and as I could not get to the prairies without a long delay I might as well start as soon as possible.

There was, however, still a long waiting list as there were Newfoundland personnel with wives and families to be brought home. Finally, I was told that April 14 was to be my sailing date. Because I knew I would be working alone, with no chance of getting a doctor in case of need, I decided to try to improve my abilities. I applied for instrumental midwifery and anesthesia training and was fortunate enough to be accepted by Dr. Annie McCall, a leading obstetrician in London and Director of the Clapham School of Midwifery, and was able to attend lectures at a large maternity hospital in London.

The training more or less specialized in training nurses for overseas and afterwards I felt more capable of facing whatever might be in store for me. One doctor for whom I had worked in Woking gave me a pair of midwifery forceps, another gave me a medical book, with a very flattering recommendation. The Mission where I had tried to help gave me a farewell party, as well as a Bible and a fountain pen. Naturally, I felt buoyed up with all this well-wishing.

So time passed quickly and now I found I was to be joined by another nurse, who had been a fellow worker at the Mission and who had recently finished training. I had gladly introduced her to Lady Harris, who had just as gladly accepted her offer of service, so we were to travel together. Then another snag. A strike was threatening in England which would have tied up all shipping so we were advised to go a day earlier. That meant sailing on Friday, April 13. We left London on April 12. Next day, we went on board the ship in Liverpool and heard the lamentations of the stevedores saying we would probably strike a mine before we had gone far.

One stevedore who sounded very Irish advised all and sundry we were committing suicide by leaving on a Friday, the 13th. "Wid all dem mines floatin' around you will sure strike one and down to the bottom you will go," he said. "Tis flying in the face of providence, dat's what it is." He was really distressed at the idea that we were, as he said, tempting providence.

Chapter 3

Newfoundland

However, nothing extraordinary happened on the crossing, excepting the usual cases of mal de mer which, as I was a good sailor, kept me very busy. A young wife, a Scottish girl married to a returned Newfoundland soldier, with a two-year-old child and a new baby about three or four weeks old was very seasick and quite incapable of attending to either herself or the children.

Stewardesses were both scarce and busy so I had every excuse to 'take over,' which I did, begging around for buckets, towels, anything usable as diapers, extra soap, everything but clothespins. But I did manage to get some safety pins, which had to do to keep laundry from blowing off into the Atlantic. Needless to say, I was not a favourite with the sailors who did not appreciate having a woman scrambling around lines and ropes to try and get laundry to dry.

My room-mate, the nurse who came with me from London, was so very seasick that she needed a lot of attention so it was a blessing I kept on my feet. Eventually it was necessary to have my friend carried up on deck and left for hours in the fresh air. She only really recovered when the ship reached port. Meanwhile, the other patient got increasingly better, the baby kept well, and I was relieved when they were all safely on shore, in the care of relatives.

We reached St. John's safely ten days later. What a lovely day it was! The clean taste of ice in the air, the frosty glitter over all the buildings and a quantity of snow still to disappear was all strange to me. I had never seen so much snow.

We were told that the preceding winter had been a very severe one, but I was to find that the next winter would be even more severe. This was especially true for a newcomer to the country like me, who had much to learn about keeping warm and dry and traveling to see patients in places where there were no roads, no vehicles, no telephone, much superstition, and sometimes reluctance to call the nurse until a greater emergency had arisen than would have been the case had a call been made earlier in the course of events.

At that time there were 83 doctors in all the island, and some were struggling for a bare existence, toiling in some regions under the harshest pioneering conditions. Along the south coast, for example, from Hermitage to Port aux Basques, lived 6,500 people without either a doctor or a nurse. One resident physician coped with the problems of an over crowded sanatorium in St. John's and the city's Mental Hospital was then without a resident doctor. A few NONA nurses did what they could to handle the medical and health situation in those regions which, through self-help, had procured their services.

In St. John's, my friend and I were met by a messenger from Government House and escorted to the YMCA building where the top floor was used as a boarding centre for females. It was here I had my introduction to Newfoundland food. I had been underfed because of the rationing system during the war years so I was astonished at the abundance of food I now saw. Two other nurses from England soon joined us and we were all kept busy with meetings at Government House and drives around St. John's in a carriage provided by Lady Harris.

Of the four of us, one went to Burgeo, one to Hant's Harbour, one to Fogo and I was sent to the Great Northern Peninsula, which was the most remote of all the districts from any kind of medical aid. This was due to the fact that I had a wider and more diversified experience and training and it was considered that I would be in a better position to deal with emergencies.

My friend and I had been posted to opposite parts of the Island, she to Joe Batt's Arm on Fogo Island and me to Daniel's Harbour, a small place on the northwest coast, facing the Gulf of St. Lawrence. It was explained to us that it would be possible to get a doctor occasionally in need at Joe Batt's Arm, but impossible in the district I was being sent to.

Lady Harris had communicated with the Rev. Thomas Greavett, the minister for this coast, asking him which, in his opinion, would be the best settlement to place me in order to give the most service to his parish. His decision was to choose Daniel's Harbour which was approximately central, so that I could be available on each end. The territory assigned to me stretched from Sally's Cove to Port aux Choix. The nearest doctor to the south was 120 miles away from Daniel's Harbour; the nearest doctor to the north was at the Grenfell Mission in St. Anthony, 163 miles away.

There were no roads. The only communication was by sea so the weather played an important part in getting to and from patients, as well as in getting supplies and mail. If the weather was too stormy the mail steamer was compelled to pass by, taking supplies and mail on the round trip, hoping to be able to land on the return trip. When this too was impossible, mail would sometimes reach me in a full mailbag, with out-of-date newspapers and letters.

Needless to say, there were often shortages of goods and medicines as a result of this isolation. There were no telephones and the post office telegraph was not in use during closed office hours so that any emergency could not be dealt with unless one happened to be on the spot, or some hardy member could go for help. If it were not too far, that could be done, but if it happened to be a long way it just had to wait.

Normally, shipping to outport communities commenced around May with the first coastal steamers leaving St. John's soon after May 1 each year. But in 1921 there was so much ice still endangering shipping that steamers were delayed. The first coastal boat to leave was the small *S.S. Susu* which took my friend, Nurse Harvey, to Fogo. I later heard the ship was caught in ice before reaching Fogo, and the crew had to use some of the provisions being freighted in order to feed the crew and passengers.

The steamer on which I was to go would be leaving Humbermouth, in the Bay of Islands on the Island's west coast, for the run along the coast to Labrador so I had to proceed by train to meet it there.

It took two days and a night to cross the Island and I was to get off the train at Curling, where I was to present Dr. Fisher with a letter of introduction written by Dr. Campbell, who had been on this coast at one time. Dr. Campbell's parting words to me were: "When you reach Daniel's Harbour there is a house there in which every occupant suffered from tuberculosis, and if it is still there you had better get it burned down."

Accommodation had been arranged for me at a hotel in Curling and there I went to find excellent clean rooms and three of four young men boarders, all of whom worked at the local bank. Now began the wait for the coastal boat to reach that side of Newfoundland.

I got bored with nothing to do, so I decided to knit some stockings which I reckoned I would need when the winter came. I read all the available reading matter and then called at the home of the doctor, begging his wife to let me help her, or to find me occupation of some sort. I had already met the doctor when I gave him my letter of introduction; he treated me courteously, but did not offer me work. His wife realized how very bored I was and took me into the house, where I helped around and eventually did a number of calls for the very over-worked doctor.

The *S.S. Home* was a small steamer which made weekly trips between Humbermouth and Battle Harbour, Labrador, taking along mail and freight, and collecting mail and freight upon the return trip. The little steamer did yeoman service and rarely passed by without having made every effort to call at all ports along the way. Its calls were of course dependent upon the weather.

During very stormy weather when it was considered too hazardous to send the mailboat ashore from the steamer, some hardy men from the community would launch a boat and go off to collect the ever welcome mail and land any passengers who wished to come ashore with them.

If it was considered risky, it was not permitted for them to land passengers, and so passengers sometimes went ashore with relatives and friends, taking their own risks. Otherwise, the passengers would have to get off at the next suitable landing place and seek accommodation there and await the return of the steamer or take advantage of any small boat which might be going to their home or, as sometimes happened, walk the distance.

The steamer finally arrived in Humbermouth, and I reached Daniel's Harbour on May 27, six weeks after I had left England. It was interesting to go along the coast, calling at each settlement, seeing mail and freight landed. Bonne Bay was beautiful and sheltered, but the other ports were only a few houses built on the shore and had no harbourage of any kind.

When the ship arrived in Cow Head, Reverend Greavett came aboard and took me ashore to see some patients. While there were some people with tuberculosis, I found that in most cases people were ill because of under-nourishment. With a plentiful supply of food and some tonic they quickly got back to normal.

Chapter 4

Daniel's Harbour

It was a beautiful smooth day when I landed in Daniel's Harbour and the inhabitants were more than usually glad to see the first steamer of the season arrive because they had been on very short rations for some time. Supplies had become short after a long and severe winter and, this time, it was an even later start than usual.

I had to wait on the steamer until I was collected by the man with whose family I was to board came and took me ashore in his boat, so I sat there watching as boxes of tinned foods were landed and it was, to me, an astonishing scene.

I was surprised to see a case of tinned corned beef being broken open and distributed. I can see now the pale but happy faces of the people as they eagerly helped to handle the freight and proceeded to roll away barrels of flour with the merchant to whom they had been consigned standing by with a pencil and a book, recording the names of the customers and hoping no doubt there would be a good fishery so that he could recover the cash.

I was yet to learn that money was a rarity, that the goods would be paid for in barter if and when the fishing season proved successful, and if and when the customers were lucky enough to catch some prime fur. I could not help contrasting the scene with the ones I had experienced in England where wholesale credit was not used this way.

My hosts, Mr. and Mrs. Moss, had arranged a bedroom and another room in their house for me to use as a clinic. The waiting room really was the kitchen, but that was fine because it was warm and roomy and the family did not mind having it used. They even enjoyed the 'visits' with their neighbours.

When people came from further away, they would come direct to the room in the front of the house. But the hospitality of these people was so great that patients were always invited to have a cup of tea before leaving. Indeed, if they lived at a distance, they were often invited to stay overnight.

At that time, there was no indoor sanitary arrangements, no running water, no sink, and so right away I had to contend with the problem of hot water, sterilization of instruments and disposal of waste. The first few weeks were hectic.

As soon as I got things straightened away, with the drugs unpacked, the patients began to arrive. Boats came from all along the shore with patients of all descriptions, some sick, some anxious, some just curious to see what this strange woman looked like. Everyone was grateful for what help and advice I could offer. People came from far and near and with everyone there was always warmth and a feeling of welcome. These people really needed someone who could help them, reassure them, and advise them.

There was plenty to keep me occupied during the first few months after my arrival. An epidemic of whooping cough was raging, and the recent shortages of food meant physical conditions were at a low standard. Boats came from outlying places, bringing patients with all sorts of different complaints, some very real, some imaginary, but all with teeth affected with cavities or decay and the resulting 'bad stomach' which had followed the tooth trouble. There was no dental chair, no anesthetic, and very few pairs of forceps.

I had brought one pair of forceps with me from England. They were called 'universal forceps' and supposed to be effective on any tooth. Alas, I found them useless. But, of course, it could have been my fearful approach due to my inexperience with extractions. Two other pairs of forceps were later supplied by the Ladies Committee in St. John's and these had to do.

Years later, when Corner Brook became a paper-making centre, I was given a number of pairs by the doctor there. He had been able to relinquish the job of tooth extractions in favour of a dentist who had commenced practice. Naturally, this enabled me to do extractions with less difficulty than before. I have been extremely lucky in that I have not had any disasters with teeth extractions, in spite of the bad state of the mouths with which I had to deal.

Before I had commenced to do extractions, the hardier people had submitted to being operated on with a wrench-like instrument, with a solid leather covered ball which fitted into the hollow of the hard palate, providing a counter pull to the part of the instrument which held the tooth. I have never seen one of these things, but patients have described it to me. It could not be sterilized, and I have often wondered if the cure of tooth extraction was not worse than the disease of decayed teeth.

The average Newfoundlander has great powers of resistance, and on occasions when they have met with axe cuts in woods work have applied gum picked from trees, and walked considerable distances to get home, in spite of the wound. Sometimes, the blood could be tracked right back to the spot where the accident happened.

That, of course, does not happen these days. Thanks to the system of road we now enjoy, people can be transported with much less delay and suffering to a hospital where up to date treatment is given and the patient is hospitalized if necessary.

There were no compensation boards in those days, and men were compelled for financial reasons to get back on the job, despite pain or discomfort.

* * * *

Superstition played a great part in the lives of the people and the one which I could never understand as having any virtue was that which was considered a certain cure for nosebleed. Merely to hang a yard of green ribbon around the victim's neck would halt the bleeding, or so they asserted.

I remember one occasion when I was attending a particularly severe post-nasal bleed, using plugs and coagulants, and hearing the patient tell her husband to go to a relative and ask him to 'charm' it, and this in absentia too. I immediately offered to go away if the charm were to be effective. My services would then not be needed. I had already stayed by for a couple of days so I would have been quite relieved if the condition could be arrested by someone somewhere reciting something. I understood a charm to consist of reading a verse in the Bible.

Needless to say, the patient and her relatives preferred my active presence and administrations to the problematical 'cure.' Eventually, the patient was removed to hospital by steamer. Patients have told me, quite seriously, that they have been relieved of toothache by having it charmed. In reality, the tooth only rots away in your head, but superstitions die hard.

Warts could be 'put away' by persons who knew how it could be done and I had some amusing experiences with warts.

I had a huge thing on the inner side of the middle finger, which bled when disturbed. I had probably got it through milking the cow. However, a neighbour saw me with a bandaged finger and asked if I had cut it.

When I told him it was a wart, he said "Oh, I will put it away for you." Of course, I thought no more of it, not believing it could be done, but it went away so gradually that I did not notice it was disappearing until one day the man asked me where the wart had been and to my astonishment I saw it was gone.

My mother-in-law also had this 'gift' and when I was relating my story to a friend over 100 miles away, she asked me to write the mother-in-law, telling her to put away some warts from the hand of her daughter.

The child was about 10 and had a mass of inter-running warts covering one thumb and spreading over the hand, so closely packed that it was impossible to count them, which I understood at the time to be a necessary part of the 'cure.'

I wrote the letter and explained why I could not give the number of the warts. Months later, my friend eagerly told me to say thank you to my mother-in-law, and insisted upon shopping for a gift for her.

Another queer idea was that when turning a boat it had to go 'with the sun.' Once, when helping to row, I tried to turn the boat the other way in order to shorten the distance somewhat, but I was sternly admonished by the fisherman who told me that they "always went the way of the sun."

So, of course, we rowed the better part of a circle to go in the way he wanted.

I soon found that there was a high incidence of tuberculosis along the coast. Educating the public was a very big problem because nobody would believe TB was an infectious disease. The sympathy of friends and relatives helped to spread the disease. They would be around with the patients and during the winter months, with big wood fires burning and windows and doors almost sealed against the weather, it followed that fresh air did not penetrate too easily not could the used air easily escape.

I myself incurred a lot of displeasure on the occasions it was necessary for me to enter a place like the post office, which was small, crowded and airless. I would stand in the open doorway to await my mail. That would prevent the closure of the door and, needless to say, nobody tried to hinder my going when I was served. It was much warmer with the door closed.

My argument that tuberculosis was infectious was met with derision. "Impossible," people would say, and quote a relative or friend who had lived with those who had died from the disease and were still well. Proof positive, they asserted, that TB was not catching!

There was no way to get patients hospitalized. The two sanatoria were at St. John's and St. Anthony, a long expensive trip for those who were sick, and probably, even if they had been able to get there, it would likely be found these hospitals were filled.

Besides, the patient would argue, they did not feel too bad. It was only the wretched cough, or the persistent fatigue, or the loss of appetite, or some other perfectly reasonable cause that made them like that. As soon as the cough gets better, or the appetite comes back, they would be alright. Anyway, they said, Nurse was TB crazy! She always wanted to hear your chest, or look down your throat or see your teeth. To even suggest anyone had TB was scandalous. It was considered a disgrace. And even when a hospital and X-ray apparatus became available patients sent by me for investigation would return without having even been to the hospital. Probably fear was a factor.

There are stories of empty bottles having been found after the death of the patient from TB, bottles under the bed or under the pillow. These empty bottles which had contained various 'cures' including such things as Friars Balsom, left sad mute evidence of the attempts to cure the disease the patient didn't have, or would not confess to having.

Chapter 5

My District

Every village in my district, which stretches along the Great Northern Peninsula, faces the Gulf of St. Lawrence and there are no inland habitations. This comes about of course because only fishing provides a livelihood so it was necessary for families to live where the livelihood was.

There were no industries of any kind and that of course helped people to be self-sufficient. Manufactured goods were difficult to obtain even if there were funds with which to buy them. So men would saw down trees and from them would build a house. Furniture was home made and sheep were kept which provided wool for clothing. The woods in the interior were hunting grounds where moose, caribou, hares and rabbits were secured for food, while seals were caught to provide both meat and skin from which sealskin boots were made. The marshlands which lie between the settlements and the forests were a good source of berries and literally gallons of cloud berries (commonly called bakeapples), marshberries, which are a kind of small cranberry, blueberries, and partridgeberries were picked and preserved.

Most families had a cow and an ox. Fresh milk, cream and butter were thus provided, while the ox was used to pull home sled loads of firewood. Because all through the fishing season there was such abundance of fresh cod, plaice, capelin, lobster and various other fish supplies, meat became almost unnecessary. Indeed, it could only be salted for preservation because there were no refrigerators, not even an icebox.

So it may be well imagined how necessary it was that people should provide against any contingency. In each settlement there was usually an older woman or man to whom the residents would look for help in accidents or sickness and these people were reliable though untrained and would spend their time and strength to help those less fortunate than themselves.

There was never any suggestion that an illegitimate child should be passed over to the Welfare Department, or to any stranger for that matter. In fact, there was no welfare department at that time... I remember old people here with no other income except their Old Age Pension, $50 per annum. Imagine. But nobody starved. People took care of their own.

In my early days, a fisherman would give me a huge fresh cod fish, or a big flat fish, or a bucket of newly dug potatoes. No payment would be accepted. No nurse had ever lived in this district so of course many people came from other places with various ailments, some minor and some serious. I was appalled by the number of decayed teeth.

No roads existed along the coast and during good weather only boats were used to get from place to place. This made for quite a lot of hardship when an emergency needed attention and one had to put off in bad windy weather in a small boat. I well remember being in a small boat enroute to a woman who had given birth a few hours previously and who now was 'having fits.'

The engine on the boat broke down and we were stranded on a choppy sea. Luckily, we had oars and eventually we reached the patient to my great relief, not to mention the relief of the patient's relatives at the arrival of help.

* * * *

It may readily be imagined that disagreements arose occasionally in those early years among those who, before my arrival, were considered, or considered themselves, authorities upon anything and everything.

One would hear of a child who had scarlet fever, only to find a nettle rash, that someone else had a lung hemorrhage only to find a gastric condition which was responsible for the bleeding.

One elderly man to whom I was called had some hemorrhage and, being persuaded that it was his lungs, set his house in order and prepared to die. It was a well known fact that such a hemorrhage only just preceded death. Upon my arrival, however, when I had examined and explained that it was just a ruptured gastric ulcer I was hardly believed. But his subsequent recovery with my medicines and diet and rest sent my stock up considerably and the man lived for many years more.

Another case of mistaken diagnosis was that of a child of around 12, who had been away from home helping at a house where there was illness. The child returned home, telling her mother she had not been too well, that she had a sore throat but was better now.

Next day, the mother noticed swollen joints and sent for me. I considered that she had been suffering from scarlet fever and advised the mother to segregate her from the rest of the family. The idea was pooh poohed, and some days later every member of that family was bedridden with scarlet fever and some were really very sick. The grandmother had evidently been immunized in her younger days because she did not succumb and was able to attend to the family. I quarantined the house and no further cases happened.

Some years later, however, a child developed a rash and the mother, fearing I would quarantine the house, kept the child out of sight until the rash disappeared. The poor child suffered ear trouble and is slightly deaf as a result.

I think of another patient who for two years had concealed a skin eruption which was obviously malignant and died when the condition developed so rapidly as to leave no way for treatment, and of another patient with acute mastitis, who was 'curing' the condition by applying a weasel skin to her breast. Her suffering caused so much distress to her husband and father that they insisted upon getting the matter attended to, and held her firmly while I made an incision to drain the pus.

Chapter 6

A Visit from the Governor, Work, Love and Marriage

Excerpts from diary Myra began in August 1921

August 26, 1921: Today I have been 'called to task' in a letter from Sister Gregory. Unintentionally it is true but she said that a diary of a life such as mine would be interesting reading in coming years 'if the person were not too lazy to write one' or similar words to that effect. Today, therefore, I commit myself unto the keeping of a diary and trust to find pleasure in the reading of it in years to come if I am spared. Three months ago I arrived at Daniel's Harbour and never for one moment since have I regretted coming. The need for medical help is beyond my power of description. The day is beautifully calm and warm. The sea is like glass and today is marked by the fact that the Governor, Sir Charles Alexander Harris, paid us a visit. The duties of 'Mayor and Corporation' rested upon my shoulders as the only 'Official' here. The men have all gone away to work on the making of a road between Deer Lake and Bonne Bay to procure the winter's provisions. I greeted the Governor upon his landing and also Captain Hamilton who accompanied him and I escorted them round the settlement and to my headquarters. A meeting was held in the schoolhouse and the Governor addressed the inhabitants. I replied in the stead of the people who were all too shy to speak. Mr. J. D. Henry spoke immediately afterwards and later embarrassed me by much praise both for my work on the coast and the 'eloquence' of my impromptu speech. I believe the Governor and his party went away pleased with the reception offered them. We found his visit most enjoyable. After the departure of the steamer I rushed back to indulge in my lovely mail, wherein was the letter that has moved me to commence this diary. Work today has been quiet, a child whose face I had to envelope in a mask – eczema, a consultation re haemorrhoids, and an insect sting complete the day so far. Now for a time on the harmonium and the day is finished. Thank God for all His mercies.

Friday, September 1: Day much calmer and brighter. A girl came in to have an aching molar extracted. Poor kid! She didn't think it much fun in spite of cocaine! A wire has just come from Port aux Choix to say a family there is very sick so I must go as soon as I get passage. I wonder what I shall find? The family I know is starving. The father isn't so dreadfully energetic! The mother died on July 13 from general septic absorption, due I think to rotten teeth, very little and poor food, lack of cleanliness etc. She was in a dreadful condition when I attended her.

Sunday, September 4: A lovely calm day and the steamer came at 8 a.m. so I had to get a move on to catch her... the sick family didn't appear so very bad and after giving advice backed up by Virol for the children and a tonic for the man, I went along to the Bretons. The usual thing happened.

Somebody wanted teeth extracted so off I went again and pulled out six for a woman. They were all she had! She was too poor to pay anything. I retired early hoping to get away early the next morning.

Friday, September 23: Directly after I had visited my patient, Mrs. Moss and I went off to pick marshberries. Oh the water! I was knee deep occasionally and got fearfully tired with the constant pulling out of the sticky mud... A dance was held at night and as Angus Bennett came for me, I went and really quite enjoyed it.

Sunday, September 25: A fine bright day. Directly after dinner Angus took me for a walk which was most enjoyable. He is such a nice man.

Tuesday, September 27: A gale is blowing. The steamer should be returning today but should the gale continue it will again pass us and carry my lovely mail on to the next port. In the afternoon I went berry picking and came home terribly tired. Directly after tea Angus came. He asked me if I would marry him... I spent a sleepless night weighing the pros and cons... I like him so much but wonder if I would make a good enough wife for a 'Colonial.' would like to settle here and continue working for these people but it means a more or less lifelong separation from my own people... Well today he has asked me again and I have consented. But I'm rather fearful for the future... Meanwhile we are keeping our engagement a secret. There will be a great surprise, I know, when it leaks out-my own people will not approve of my settling here. Anyway, I am not free to marry until April 1923 and anything may happen between now and then so I agree with Angus that for the present anyway secrecy will be best. We are planning to get married somewhere away from here to avoid fuss and ceremony and the endless chatter that will result when people get an inkling that I am to marry. Meanwhile Angus will go on housebuilding and preparing and I shall go on quietly working.

Monday, October 17: A perfectly gorgeous day. Sun shining brilliantly although it is fairly cold... During the evening Angus came up and wrote to father to ask for me. Then I was called away to F. B. who was almost suffocated with bronchitis. It meant hard work for awhile. Eventually I returned home accompanied by Reverend Greavett, the Anglican minister greatly to Angus's chagrin. He was glum all evening and finally departed before Reverend Greavett.

* * * *

Angus was the oldest of ten children born to John William and Ann Keziah Benoit of Daniel's Harbour on March 15, 1897. Angus' father was from the southwest coast of Newfoundland and of French origin. His mother was the daughter of James Guinchard, a French soldier in the Crimean War. Guinchard had been awarded the Victoria Cross by the British government after he saved the lives of three British officers and the story goes that he was on the street recovering from his wounds when he was snatched up by a press gang and put on a fishing boat bound for Newfoundland. Somewhere on the west coast he managed to escape. He ended up in Daniel's Harbour where he married one of the daughters of James Biggin, the first settler in that place. Biggin's daughter, Ann Keziah, married John William Benoit. When their son, Angus, married Myra Grimsley she refused to have the name Benoit on the marriage certificate as she wanted her children to be British so the name was changed to Bennett.

Myra first met Angus when she attended the birth of his mother's tenth and last child on August 12, 1921. At that time, Angus had been away since May 1913 when he joined a ship at age 16. He had been at sea for seven years, four as a merchant marine during the First World War. When he arrived back in Daniel's Harbour he had $800 in the Bank of Montreal in Curling, the only bank in the region. That money would assist him in building a house, buying twine to make nets, and constructing a boat for fishing.

Myra was supposed to remain single and devote her life to nursing according to the terms of her contract, but she broke the contract in order to marry Angus. The couple wed in the school chapel in Daniel's Harbour on January 26, 1922. On the marriage certificate he is listed as being 24, a bachelor and a fisherman. Myra was 29, a spinster and a trained nurse. They were married in a Church of England ceremony by Reverend Greavett. Alex and Mildred Bennett, Angus' brother and sister, were the witnesses. After the wedding, the newlyweds went to the groom's home for a wedding breakfast of baked beans and cocoa. The mother-in-law's gift to the bride was a duck feather bed, a nightstand and some blankets.

Angus was a seaman, a fisherman, a trapper, a carpenter and a shop-keeper/entrepreneur. His endeavours included selling lumber, fish, furs, tinned bakeapples, tinned rabbit and tinned lobster. Angus went to school until he was nine and in grade three. He quit then and went to work, fishing in the summer, on his father's fur trap line in the winter and going to sea to earn a living at age sixteen.

Angus went on to become a successful businessman who was known for his generosity. His reaction when someone asked was he going to charge a certain man for stealing a 100-pound bag of flour from him was to say, "No, he is a poor man and badly needed the food for his family. I shall give him another bag of flour; this bag of flour he won't have to steal." Angus was also a husband and father and, for the more than 70 years of his marriage to Myra, he was an irreplaceable component of the couple known affectionately all along the coast as The Nurse and Angus.

Throughout their long and harmonious marriage, Angus sailed a boat for Myra, took charge of her dog team, harnessed the horse, and was her right-hand man when their kitchen became an operating center. Sometimes Angus would stay home and keep house while Myra went down the coast on some extended errand of mercy. He always insisted he was wonderful lucky that he could help a woman like Myra.

A daughter, Grace Eveline, was born to Angus and Myra on August 27, 1923. On September 3, 1926, they had a son they named Trevor, and on June 24, 1930, another daughter they called Barbara. In addition to raising a family of three, Angus and Myra also fostered four other children.

* * * *

From The Daily Mail
London, England, July, 1921
An English Nurse
Sir A. Harris's story of an unofficial welcome

Sir Alexander Harris, ex-governor of Newfoundland, speaking at the Royal Colonial Institute, Northumberland Avenue, said the Englishwoman could be as good a pioneer as ever was any of the old navigators.

During an official tour in Newfoundland he called at Daniel's Harbour, an isolated settlement on a long stretch of coast, which was the headquarters of a nurse sent to the district by his wife's committee. The following is his account.

When we arrived a small crowd awaited us. We were received not by a magistrate or policeman, or any usual representative of authority, but by a bright-looking nurse in full uniform, looking as if she had just come out of the wards of St. Thomas's Hospital.

Most of the leading men of the little place were away on some distant fishery, probably the Labrador. Those who were left behind were shy and awkward, and huddled behind the nurse in some doubt as to that strange being, a Governor whom they had never seen before.

It was the nurse who offered an impromptu address of welcome. It was the nurse who marshaled a procession to the schoolroom, and it was she who also returned a speech of thanks to my address, and very well Miss Grimsley did it.

Chapter 7

Life in Newfoundland

The inhabitants of the outports of Newfoundland are peculiarly fortunate in that their expenses are so low. Very little has been levied from the outport person except for the social security assessment tax, and that has only been in effect during the past few years when money replaced barter and work was available. Outport men own their own homes with no benefit from mortgage help. They only needed to select a site, clear it of trees if trees were there, and then proceed to get the materials to build the dwelling. The wood was there for the felling and sawing, so only the labour was required to build a house.

If he worked well, he would erect a home, fence around it, put in crops, keep a cow or a horse, maybe both, and with a few hens would have a good start in life. If he were married, it was the usual procedure for the young couple to live with the parents for awhile, until the man would see his way clear to setting up a separate home.

This was a very good practice inasmuch that if the bride did not prove too good a housekeeper, mother-in-law could and usually did stimulate the young woman to a better performance of her duties than might have been given with no supervision. Usually the girls were very good workers, anxious to show off their accomplishments.

But of course in every class, a lazy person does show up occasionally, who would be willing to let mother do it. Sometimes the older woman may acquiesce and do more than her share of chores especially if the younger woman is pregnant, but when mother-in-law is convinced that daughter-in-law is shirking, she has her method of putting things in order. This usually takes the form of dividing up the duties and allocating them – such as separating the items for washing, instead of doing it all at once in the one tub.

The floors to be scrubbed would be divided in sections and I have seen kitchens with beautifully scrubbed floors with a strip left dirty the length of the room. That was daughter-in-law's section, so what else could daughter-in-law do, but to get to work and scrub it and try to equal the milky whiteness of mother-in-law's section. But when the daughter-in-law was in bed with the first, or any baby, mother-in-law was the devoted nurse and nothing was left undone that would contribute to the comfort of the young mother, her husband and any other children.

When the young husband had decided to commence his own home, he would proceed to get the lumber and haul the trees to a sawmill. This would probably be owned by another man, and together they would rip the boards, the mill owner taking half the lumber as payment for the use of the mill and the gasoline and labour he had expended. Relatives and friends would help to put down the foundation of the house. Payment was not usually discussed, but it was considered that a similar helping hand on the part of the builder would recompense the helpers when they in turn needed such assistance.

Glass for the windows, nails, roofing, paint and putty, were usually obtained through the merchant, who had probably supplied fishing gear and would be willing to wait until the end of the fishing season for payment – if the season had proven successful. This credit system has been vigorously condemned in recent years, the supposition being that the merchant could charge as much as they liked and usually did, so that when the fisherman did put in his earnings for credit against his bill there was never enough to clear up his indebtedness.

I think this is very unfair. It often happened that the merchant did not get paid as much as he had paid for the cost of the goods he had supplied and one hears of merchants who went bankrupt as a result of extending credit to men who would not pay if they had a good season. I myself have known of men who, although able to buy and pay for all the necessities for fishing, would not risk their own money, but would rather accept the goods from the merchant and settle for them at the end of the fishing season, if they had secured enough fish.

If it so happened that insufficient fish had been caught to meet the required amount, the merchant had to wait until the next year and hope to be reimbursed then, but the fisherman would still expect to be again supplied with goods for the season. I must say that, by and large, I found the fishermen with whom I came into contact both eager and willing to pay their way. They would proudly tell of having squared off for the year and if there was enough coming to them after accounts had been settled, would not accept the money, but lay in the winter's necessities.

I have heard of men who had used the last cent of earnings with which to settle their bills, and in so doing had been left with absolutely nothing for the purchase of the winter stock. But miraculously something would turn up. A valuable pelt would be caught, which would bring in enough to buy supplies for a time and last while the man went again to inspect his traps.

I know of one man who had ten children to support and who had given his entire earnings to the merchant as payment for his fishing supplies, leaving himself with no money for the winter. He went looking for pearls. Not too far away there was a brook where clams were procured for bait, and occasionally a pearl would be found. After spending considerable time digging and opening clams, he was rewarded with such a perfect pearl that its sale provided enough food for the whole winter.

And so other men in those days made ends meet and with fishing and hunting and growing vegetables never went hungry, although of course there were no luxuries. Scarcity of money did not seem to worry people too much. They had never been used to having much to use and the barter system satisfied their needs.

The dried fish, tinned lobster, tinned rabbits and furs all were given in exchange for the things the people could not provide for themselves, such as flour, molasses, sugar, tea, beans and peas. There would be a supply of marshberries and bakeapples put by in their fresh state for winter use, with plenty of wild raspberry jam. Rabbit and moose meat were usually available for the catching, and made a tasty addition to the diet during the winter months. Milk and butter came from their own cows as well as the occasional carcass of mutton from their sheep. All this did not call for expenditure of money.

While the winter months were spent by the men hunting and securing the supply of firewood for the year, the women would be busy in the homes at spinning, knitting, mat hooking and making skin boots for the family. Making homespun pullovers and cardigans, stockings and caps for all the children and stockings and mitts for the men, as well as long underwear, kept them occupied. The long home-knit underwear the men wore kept them snug while trapping, and helped them withstand the cold of spring fishing.

Cod livers and seal fat and any scraps of fat or oil were saved and converted to homemade soap by the women and it was customary to see slabs of this soap spread to dry in the sun. It was excellent for cleaning and of course quite cheap. Toilet soap was only used for personal requirements, but I have regretted the passing of the homemade soap.

Since the 'improvement' in the standard of living, and the use of washing machines, with the consequent use of powdered soap and detergents, I have had very many cases of skin irritation.

Because the mothers did not realize the condition as being a direct result of the residue of these soap powders left in clothing, they would try to cure the condition by application of various salves, with a bad dermatitis finally spreading over the body. After many cases, and much explanation of what I considered the causative agent, the condition became less common. My theory was that some bleaching agent had been left in the clothing which, when released by perspiration or other wetting agents, set up an irritation. This would induce scratching, which in turn made tiny abrasions, opening up the way for infection of the skin. A vicious circle was thus set in motion and it took quite some talking and comparison of cases to get the parents to understand.

With the use of mild acid solutions, the condition would clear up and, needless to say, when it was demonstrated to the parents the miraculous speed with which the condition cleared up when the antidote was applied the problem disappeared. I did have one case of a child who for two years had a mild dermatitis which did not respond to treatment. Eventually, I discovered that the mother had used an antiseptic soap exclusively for the child since its birth. Discontinuance of the particular soap saw the end of the skin condition.

My early years were a daily round of common tasks, so many carious teeth to be extracted, so many bad stomachs, epidemics of influenza, of mumps, of measles, and the large number of accidents, some of which might have been avoided with a little thought.

I found myself talking and talking, teaching and teaching, explaining preventive measures demonstrating causes and effects. But I too learned so much, how to card and spin wool and knit garments for my children and how to make and mend skin boots. In return, I taught things like sewing and renovating, cooking and dieting, and, most of all, the uselessness of the superstitions which had such a hold on the imaginations of the people.

* * * *

When I was able to visit the other settlements, I found I needed to make arrangements for expectant mothers. With so much territory to cover, it was impossible to run from one to another at opposite poles, if more than one woman was in labour, not to mention daily care of mother and baby.

So when people began to realize the benefit of trained care, I had no difficulty in persuading them to come and stay with friends or relatives in Daniel's Harbour so that I could attend to several in a shorter time, and not leave anyone untended. Of course this too caused some resentment among a few of the older women who had hitherto conducted the cases. But it was not long before everyone came around to my way of thinking.

Although the practice of midwifery was my chief love, there was still a lot of general work to be done. With no possibility of getting dental care, there were very few mouths in good condition and consequently many many persons suffered with "stomach" trouble. Impetigo persisted, scabies persisted, chiefly because it was a 'disgraceful' disease and was hidden. Then there were numbers of axe cuts, trout hooks embedded in places where they should not be – always a call of some kind, regardless of time of day or night.

Meanwhile, my own home was being built. It was a slow process, with very little cash, no trained workmen, and the need for earning a living while building. I was often away for weeks on end, staying in different settlements, having gone in the first place in response to an emergency call or a baby case and stayed to help the patient get on her feet again, look after the family, attend to various conditions in the neighbourhood, do some health visiting, tooth extractions, etc.

When I left, I usually had a notebook written up with the needs of the patients, which I would attend to when I reached home. Packages of medicines would then be sent to the patient with instructions and then after a few days at home I would be off again, probably in the other direction.

* * * *

I found the people very co-operative and helpful. When it is realized that these people had never had any tuition in anything but manual labour and only had been educated in the three R's and not much of that, it is no wonder that they substituted superstition and charms to help with the ills of life.

Outside news only reached them through the local post office, where pages were written by the postmaster, who had copied news from the telegraph line from St. John's. Then, somebody who could read would explain to the best of his ability what was happening in the world; and even this "news" was limited by the reader's understanding and ability to explain where things were happening.

Earnings were so small that as soon as a boy or girl could get a job off they had to go, no more schooling for them. The boy would have to help catch and cure fish and the girl would have to become a helper in a household, where probably there was a large family or there was a new baby expected.

Usually, at twelve years of age, a girl could make bread, do a family wash on the washboard, knit socks and mitts, spin wool, and help to plant and harvest vegetables. They certainly worked. Occasionally the job would only last a month and the payment might be a pair of shoes or a dress.

It was time for improvement and, to my way of thinking, only the opening of this section of the island by roads and better communication would help with the expansion of interests, educational opportunities, and general knowledge.

I suppose that, during the first twenty years or more of my life in Newfoundland, I put more thorns in the sides of the powers-that-be with my demands and suggestions for roads and communications than any other person in the country.

Never did I think I would enjoy these benefits, it was too much to expect, considering conditions, finances, etc. But maybe my efforts might result in better conditions for my children and grandchildren, so that they might not have to undergo the misery and inconvenience we older ones had experienced and eventually having to leave their country to obtain better conditions.

Chapter 8

My Kitchen Cases

Traveling took up so much time in my early days on the coast. Settlements were separated by distance as well as intervening streams, bogs, ponds, and only in hard winter was it possible to proceed over frozen terrain or frozen water, either with a team of dogs or a horse and sled or on foot.

But somehow or other, I was always able to reach the patient. Sometimes the patient would reach me first, as on the occasion when I was just about to leave a settlement for home when a lad standing behind a horse got a full kick in the face from an iron shod hoof.

His teeth were knocked out, his lower lip torn away and his face fairly pulverized. The only thing to do was to take him on my sled and get him to my home as quickly as possible. He was bedded in my kitchen, his face stitched up as well as I could, which was not too well because the tissues were so badly torn that stitches did not hold. I had to approximate the pieces, bind them as well as possible, leaving a small hole through which a straw could pass in order to feed him on fluids.

He did well, and after a few weeks he was fit to proceed to hospital, where I sent him because the hard palate showed a separation, and I hoped a surgeon would be able to unite it and permit him to have a dental plate inserted. He spent some time in the hospital and finally was returned to me, with the request that I would extract a tooth which was bothering him. He made a good recovery, had a good dental fitting and remarkably little scarring.

At this time, I had a cow which supplied us with milk and butter. She had calved and the calf staggered under the belly of a large horse we had in the barn. A man went in search for the calf and frightened the horse which lashed out, throwing the man against the wall of the barn, where he came into contact with the ladder reaching to the loft. One of the rungs of the ladder had ripped the scalp across the head from ear to ear, laying open the skull. Instinctively, he grabbed at a handful of snow and put it against the skull while he ran to the house for my help. The injury did not scare me as much as the fact that he had used the dirty snow to apply to the open wound, and I had no anti-tetanus serum. I was terribly afraid of tetanus.

However, putting him on the kitchen settle, I washed and shaved the scalp and stitched it back in its original position, gave the poor man a shot of rum seeing as I had no anesthetic, bound him up and hoped for the best.

I am sure I did not sleep for several days, expecting to be called at any moment to see this patient but, thankfully, his condition never gave me a moment's anxiety. Had the operation been performed in a proper theatre, it could not have healed better. But it was only after a considerable time had elapsed that my fears vanished.

* * * *

My kitchen was the scene of many minor operations I had to undertake in emergencies, such as when a lad was brought in with a deep axe cut through the instep, needing several stitches and I had to post a guard at the door to prevent a hysterical mother from coming in to see the lad and preventing me from suturing the foot.

One day a dog team brought a man who was suffering from a badly infected arm. He told me that he had been bitten on the elbow by what he thought was a spider. The wound became septic, and in spite of his treatment at home the infection had now travelled up and down until the whole arm was swollen from finger tips to shoulder blade.

He was in extreme pain, with a high temperature, and the long sleigh ride over bumpy territory had not done much to ease his condition. He was unable to rest in any position and the arm was stiff and extended. I 'hospitalized' him on my kitchen couch.

After making him as comfortable as possible, I proceeded to the task of evacuation of some of the pus which had accumulated in the tissues. Several incisions were made and the amount of discharge was almost unbelievable. It was necessary to use newspapers which could be burned to drain off the stream into containers. For some days the seepage continued and eventually it was possible to insert drains connecting the various incisions, thus eliminating various pockets of discharges.

As his temperature subsided and he could take nourishment in better quantities his strength returned and his arm became mobile and he was at last able to get up and around and take an interest in his surroundings. Finally there remained only a small spot at the original site of the infection. This was at the elbow and it seemed to defy all my attempts to get it closed so when navigation opened and the coastal boat commenced its run I arranged for him to proceed to the Grenfell Hospital at St. Anthony.

This journey takes five days given good weather, so I supplied dressings for the arm and sent an accompanying letter describing the onset and treatment of the condition. I stated that I feared some bone involvement at the elbow joint which was causing the wound to remain open.

Upon his arrival at the hospital the wound had practically healed, but I was glad he had gone for examination. Maybe I had been too anxious about the elbow and the enforced rest with nobody fussing about it during the trip was all it needed. He made a complete recovery, and as a thank you offering he made me a cedar top table to demonstrate how he could use the arm.

A similar case was that of a three-month-old baby who had an infection of the thigh. When I first saw the child I evacuated about a pint of pus and after a while the child was returned to its home. The condition returned some weeks later, but this time the whole body had been invaded and the poor child assumed an S like position with large abscesses on thigh and abdomen. Literally pints of pus had to be drained off before the child could be transported to hospital. Once there, the baby became the pet of the whole staff. In time, he was cured and developed into a happy healthy normal child.

* * * *

One very cold day in winter, a dog team arrived with a man who had been in the bunk for several days at a logging camp. He was brought in and put on my kitchen day bed. He was unconscious and so swollen that his eyes could not open.

I found almost solid urine upon testing, a sure sign of severe kidney infection. I had no other place to nurse him but my kitchen and the nearest hospital at St. Anthony was too far away to take him.

At that time my house was being built and I had only two rooms, one where Angus and I slept, and my kitchen which was used for everything else. During the six weeks the poor man spent in my kitchen he had to see tooth extractions and minor accidents dealt with while ante-natal cases of women needing examination were seen to in my bedroom.

When the man's condition had improved sufficiently that he was able to be up and about, I sent him home with instructions to go to hospital at the first opportunity. I heard later that the improvement was maintained and he did not consider it necessary to go for further treatment or advice. Not long after this, another man was brought in with TB meningitis. His mother came and collected him, declaring she would not let him die but, alas, he did.

* * * *

An emergency situation arose in February 1926 when Alex, my husband's 22-year-old brother, slipped under a circular saw at the woods camp where he was working and had his ankle sawn through with only an inch of instep holding the foot.

The men on the scene had picked him up from under the saw, taken him to the camp, suspended the leg by a rope from the roof then came for me. Angus threw the harness on Kit and we set off on the four mile trip to the camp over snowy bumpy unmade roads. It was dark and we were tangling with trees and backing and going forward on a trip that seemed endless.

At last we reached Alex and found him in shock but still conscious. We brought him home. In my kitchen, with the help of neighbours, I cleaned the wound. Alex was in a state of shock so I couldn't give him an anesthetic, and he had nothing to dull the pain as I picked out the scraps of bone and the bits of sealskin boot and the scraps of wool from the homespun socks which had been driven into the wound by the ¼-inch saw teeth. When I had removed all I could possibly get, I stitched the foot back on the leg.

My neighbours sewed up bags made from lint and filled them with snow which we packed around the leg. The snow filled bags helped anesthetize the leg and helped reduce the intensity of the pain. We could do nothing more then, and had to wait out the night until the post office would be open and we could send for help. I knew this was a job for a surgeon.

The nearest doctor at that time was a private practitioner at Bonne Bay. As soon as the post office opened next morning, I telegraphed asking him if he could possibly get here.

His reply was that we had better take Alex to Bonne Bay so we prepared to set forth. This was February, and a very heavy snowfall had left several feet of snow, through which we would have to try to drive a heavy sleigh on which we put a feather bed for the patient. I had splinted the leg, immobilizing it as much as possible. Thinking we would have less depth of snow to push through, we decided to go out to sea and maybe get a smoother run over the drifting ice. There was not much difference.

It was a dreadful journey. The poor horse would sink to its haunches in the snow, then try to jump out, causing distress to the patient. The fact that the telegraph line went through all the other post offices en route was rather a favour because the operators in each place heard the message I had sent, also the reply from the doctor, and were watching out for us.

We went ashore at Parsons Pond, to look for better going and there we found that a team of men were waiting for us. They carried Alex up a 50-foot bank with great care and then pulled the heavy sleigh up. Others helped Angus and I.

We were brought to the house of Mrs. William Isaac Payne, an alert telegraph operator in Parsons Pond. Mrs. Payne, the first telegraph operator when telegraphy was introduced on the coast, had heard my message and immediately began organizing a team of helpers along the trail.

She now instructed her helpers to take the horse out of the shafts, put it in her barn, feed it and help generally. It was too late to proceed and indeed the horse could not have gone much further, it was exhausted. Angus and I were also very tired, having had to walk the journey and help lift and twist the heavy sleigh when it got into difficulties in ice and snow. Mrs. Payne had placed a bed on the floor, had a huge pot of soup on the stove, and was prepared to house us for the night.

Mrs. Payne insisted upon sitting up with Alex while I got some rest. But, naturally, I could not expect to rest while he was in such distress. Nevertheless, the rest and food with which we were greeted helped us considerably.

Next morning we resumed the journey and this time got as far as Sally's Cove, where again we were welcomed and taken into the home of Mrs. Edna Roberts. She gave us food and sleeping quarters for the night, and all this with no thought of recompense, nor would any offer of payment have been accepted.

The horse was fed and placed in a warm barn, and next morning again we set forth on the last lap of the journey, this time across the frozen bay. I must confess that here I was rather scared. Crossing a large expanse of water with a heavy horse, sleigh and feather bed, plus three pedestrians, was certainly a new experience for me. But, fortunately, nothing untoward occurred and we reached the house which had been arranged to be our headquarters and wherein the doctor was able to visit the patient daily.

As it happened, the doctor did not have to undo any of the work I had done on the leg, nor add to anything, but the fact that he was now in charge of the case and could supply drugs and dressings was a great comfort to me.

We stayed there a few weeks. My husband had to return home, leaving us to come when conditions warranted. Alex made a good recovery, though for some time there would appear a little local irritation when a scrap of foreign matter (skin or wool) would appear and be removed from the wound.

Had that accident happened today, it would have taken only a half hour or so to have Alex brought to hospital, where he would have the benefit of a capable doctor, trained personnel and an operating theatre always ready for emergencies.

But in this case it took us three days and two nights to accomplish the trip. Both nights we stayed at homes prepared to receive us and we had the best that could be offered at each home. When we finally reached the doctor we had to find a lodging where we stayed not too far from his home. But, by that time it was only a matter of supervision on the part of the doctor and an immense relief to me to have a superior in charge.

After a few weeks near the doctor we again left for home, where I continued to attend Alex until he could get about on crutches. Finally, there was complete healing and he could walk on the foot which had been all but severed. I shall never forget the kindness shown to us nor the hospitality given us on that occasion; it certainly helped to take so much distress and unhappiness from us. This behaviour attended me all through the years of my work in Newfoundland. I never experienced so much thought for others, and so spontaneously given.

* * * *

In another instance, when I was called to a maternity case thirty miles away, and it was necessary for me to take my small daughter, Grace, just ten months old, for want of someone with whom I could leave her for an indefinite time, I set forth in a boat, together with an old lady of 70 from Daniel's Harbour who wished to go to the same place to visit her daughter.

She packed a cold fried herring and some bread in a bag and we set forth. We got as far as Bellburns when stormy weather compelled us to go ashore and pull up the boat. There was no way to get to the patient except by foot so several young people offered to walk with us, dividing the luggage among them, taking turns at carrying my child, a bundle of necessities for her and my midwifery bag.

Bellburns was only seven miles from Daniel's Harbour so there were still 23 miles to go to get to my patient. After some time we reached a woodsman's camp at Point au Fountain, deserted but with some kindling left for travellers and a stove and an empty kettle. It was the rule that anyone using the camp would replenish the kindling and wood so that no weary traveller would be without warmth. So the lads brought in splits and logs while the girls lit the fire and I undressed my baby.

I found her legs extremely cold. I had not realized that the keen wind would blow through her woolen clothing and as her legs had not been protected by my body they had received the brunt of the icy wind.

However, with a good fire and some massaging and heated clothing she was soon restored to normal and I had learned another of the thousands of lessons so necessary for such a greenhorn as me.

The herring and bread was divided and eaten between us; remembering the bible story of the five loaves and two small fishes? But it tasted good. Having carefully smothered the fire with snow, in case a spark set fire to the cabin, we again took our loads and walked on.

After a while we were pleasantly surprised to see some men approaching who had come to meet us, and who had a boat to take us across the bay.

The patient was a woman about to give birth to her first child. She had recently come from England, married in St. John's, and came to take up residence on this coast with her husband, who was a Customs officer.

What I did not know was that before coming to Newfoundland she had spent two years in a frame for some spinal disability and nobody seemed to realize this would alter the shape of her pelvis and so cause difficulty in childbirth.

The labour and delivery was a nightmare! With no hospital and no means of transportation, it was impossible to get her to where she could have a Caesarian operation so I was compelled to act as best I could.

It was quickly apparent that only instrumental delivery would produce the child. I was able to get the help of a woman who had done some deliveries before any qualified midwives were available in Newfoundland and she gave the anesthetic for me while I applied forceps.

With the greatest difficulty I managed to deliver the tiny four pound eight ounce baby, alive. The child's face had the half serious appearance sometimes seen in forceps deliveries. It is caused by pressure on a nerve but soon clears up.

The child's father was very distressed because only half of the face puckered up when she cried. The distress was unfounded because the normal side did pucker up while the other side remained bland and beautiful and that was the side he preferred.

He was even more distressed when I assured him that as the condition improved both sides would pucker up. He did not like that idea at all. He would have liked the normal side to be as beautiful as the other side. The child grew up to be a lovely looking girl with no facial blemish of any kind.

* * * *

It was on another trip, this time by dog team on the ice off shore after I had been collected by men from Port Saunders to attend a baby case there, that we were intercepted by a few men as we crossed by River of Ponds. They hailed us, asking us to go ashore to see a sick child.

Naturally the men who had come for me refused, seeing they were in a hurry to get to the patient awaiting their arrival. With no more ado the other men just took the dogs by the harness and dragged them ashore. They said they would hold them there until I had seen the sick child.

When I saw the child, I was rather glad they had done this. The baby had a distended abdomen and was obviously in great pain. The mother explained that the baby would not suck because every time it tried to feed it would scream, therefore, the child's throat must be the cause. Seeing the distension was caused by retention of gas and thinking of the peristalsis, or muscle contractions, which sucking would set up it was not to be wondered at that the child refused to suck. I decided that irrigation would expel the gas so set up arrangements.

Taking the child across my knees I gave the baby a warm washout. The poor little mite! I hated letting the maternity patient wait for me. But how could I leave this baby in such agony for the indefinite time it would take to complete the journey, not to mention the time taken to complete the delivery which, after all, might not be too imminent.

It was not too long before the baby's condition improved and the abdomen slackened in its tenseness. The child was again able to suck ravenously without pain. I was so thankful the men had the courage to insist on getting help for the baby. The maternity patient was not too distressed at the delay and that case was successfully completed too. Upon the return trip to my home, I called upon the family and saw the baby, quite happy with no recurrence of the trouble.

A less happy incident happened during a walk I was taking in the spring when the pond and small "flashets" were beginning to thaw. My object was to get some inoculations done so I was walking briskly along and jumping from one icy patch to another. I jumped short at one small flashet, my foot went through the ice at the edge. The heel caught in a submerged root and the instep brought up against the hard edge of the ice covering the tiny pond.

I had to pull my foot out of the long skin boot I was wearing, get the boot out of the water, then get the injured foot back in the boot and carry on. I had to get the inoculations done and then limp the rest of the way home. I was thankful there were no broken bones or dislocations. I was able to bandage the foot and after a rest I was as good as new.

* * * *

Fractures were my greatest worry. But, nevertheless, occasionally I would have to deal with them. My husband was returning from a neighbouring settlement during the freeze-up when the ponds were not too well hardened. He was trying to jump across a small pond when he slipped at the edge which gave way causing him to fall and break a forearm. His companion held the arm while they all walked a good distance. It must have been extremely painful. Luckily I had plaster of paris and set the bones to the best of my ability and put the arm in plaster. There was no way to get him to hospital as the coastal steamer had ceased running for the winter months, and the ground and streams were not sufficiently frozen to bear a team. So, he had to endure until the opening of navigation in May, when I sent him for an X-ray and correction of the setting if necessary. I might have known better. He returned after having completed some business, but had not gone to the hospital. I never did know if the setting was as accurate as I wished but the arm has never given any trouble. It united well so it must have been comparatively correct.

Another fracture was that of a femur in a young school girl. She had been leaving the school building when a rush of children behind her pushed her down and other children fell on her, breaking the leg midway between knee and thigh. When she was brought home the only place to attend her was the hard wooden settle in the kitchen. There I got the leg in as good alignment as possible while the child's father made a long splint to my instructions. At that time, there was no hospital nearer than St. John's on one side and St. Anthony on the other. Both would have taken a week or so to reach. However, having strapped the splint into position, I used a bag of beach rocks as weights to keep the leg extended. I nursed the child in the kitchen, visiting at least twice a day, and worrying in case of a tilted pelvis resulting. Happily, she made a good recovery and in later years married, had children normally, and is now a grandmother.

Chapter 9

Early Years

Daniel's Harbour is so named because a man named Daniel who was sailing with his family from Forteau, Labrador, to Bonne Bay sought shelter there during a storm sometime prior to 1830.

He must have had a small boat because no large ship could get anywhere near the place. In spite of its name, Daniel's Harbour has no harbour, with the exception of a few large rocks behind which small boats could be lashed on in case of a storm.

For all of us living in Daniel's Harbour in the 1920s, the steamer's calls became a social gathering at the beach. Everyone would gather there to see who had come as well as what had come. In September, there would be the new teacher, and in June there would be the departure of the teacher. The men would have their boats and dories out in the stream ready to approach the steamer as soon as the anchor had let go. They would get alongside and accept the freight, row it ashore, dump it on the beach, and return for another load again and again until it had all been landed. Then there would be the sorting out, the placing in stores of food for various owners, the heavy puncheons of molasses rolled up above high watermark, the barrels of salt beef and pork as well as tanks of kerosene put away safely.

Motor boats were just being introduced for fishing and a couple of 3-hp motors were in use so there was not much call for gasoline at that time. As most adults wore skin boots and the children wore skin moccasins there was no call for stocks of footwear. Indeed there was no money to buy them, so seals were caught, the skins tanned and used in the home to make footwear.

I must confess that I preferred to use skin boots. They were light in weight, warm and comfortable, waterproof, and could be made and repaired at home. To me it was an ideal way to dress. One could walk tirelessly for miles, regardless of wet or dry or frozen terrain. One could wade ashore from boats, one could spend days in the wet marshes and pick the delicious marshberries without getting either wet or cold feet. Of course, home spun and knit stockings helped to keep the feet comfortable too, and although modern ideas have contributed to the disuse of skin boots, I am glad to say that homespun wool is still used, although not in so great a quantity as it used to be.

How bright and cheerful the homes were. The fact that shops were practically non existent resulted in the housewife brightening up her home by her own devices. No garments were ever discarded; they were remade over and over and handed down to smaller members of the family. In the remaking, the cuttings were kept, dyed and used for the lovely hooked rugs.

In almost every kitchen during the long winter evenings there would be a mat frame in use. Sometimes a small party would join in completing a mat for one house, and proceed to help with another at another house, each vying with friends to produce new designs and colours. Paint was too expensive to be much use so floors and surroundings were scrubbed white. The mats added a cheerful bright note.

The women were industrious and would be seen on the beaches, sleeves rolled up, wearing long rubber or skin boots, helping their men to prepare the catch of codfish for the salting down process. They would cut out the cod tongues, and the edible parts of the heads, which in turn were salted away for winter food. In my ignorance, I first thought these things were not too nice. But I have not only changed my mind, I prefer some of these foods to many others of a more familiar nature. They make delicious eating, are nourishing, and naturally very cheap.

Later on, my husband and I were to develop a market for tinned cod tongues. It was amusing, at one time, when I had a crowd of hungry men in for dinner that I was compelled to fall back on some tinned goods. It was a Friday and of course one does not ask for the religious beliefs of visitors so I steered the way by providing both meat and fish for them. The fish consisted of tinned cod tongues, and I explained that those who preferred fish could help themselves, while those who cared for meat could also help themselves. The cod tongues disappeared as if by magic. The meat stayed. I never did know what the religious beliefs were, but evidently everyone was a Newfoundlander who liked cod tongues.

Newfoundland people are notoriously hospitable. It did not matter whether one arrived during daylight hours, or after dark, the welcome was always warm and sincere. Of course there were occasions when it was quite inconvenient to put up a traveller. Perhaps there was sickness in the house. Perhaps a new baby had recently made its appearance.

But, but by and large, it was only necessary to knock on a door, to be bidden to enter and be made at home. If accommodation were limited, arrangements would be made so that a bed would be available for the unexpected guest and he or she would be given the best the house could offer. In those days, sometimes the best was not too good, or it might happen that the lunch I carried along in case of need would be consumed by the children where I had put up for the night.

Hospitality was always extended to travellers. Payment was never suggested, possibly because there was no money anyway. The traveller would get the best that could be provided under the circumstances.

In spite of abject poverty, the welcome was always warm and soon after one's arrival a few neighbours would trickle in to hear the 'news.' This sometimes became rather embarrassing from my point of view.

People did not understand any need for my reticence in discussing conditions I had treated professionally, nor for privacy in dealing with patients. However, they would be quite reasonable about it when I would ask them to leave me alone with the patient.

Tooth extractions were, of course, not a matter for privacy, and sometimes a kitchen would be the scene of operations with the about to be patients joking with the ones who were undergoing extractions. I think the atmosphere was wholesome. The onlookers kept up the morale of the patients, and we had no bother.

There was quite a bit of tuberculosis, carious teeth and malnutrition, and although this sounds rather dreadful, there was so much reason for these conditions that it gave me a great deal of hope that things could be rectified if I got the confidence and co-operation of the people.

Education was the first goal. How I talked. It was uphill work because nobody could imagine a disease could be infectious when no spots or outward signs were there to show what was wrong. Therefore, TB became enemy Number One, and I found that sympathetic friends did not like to be told that they ran a risk by sitting with open cases of the disease

Decayed teeth were a problem too. But people were so anxious to get the bad teeth removed that they submitted to my amateur dental efforts, and this was so effective that years later when the Red Cross Society sent qualified dentists to see the school children, I was complimented upon the healthy mouths encountered here.

Bad stomachs were the order of the day, but with improved dental conditions and a more varied diet they get less and less frequent, and today I hear very little about bad stomachs unless someone has overeaten.

The question of malnutrition was more easily overcome. When I first arrived, people had become malnourished because of the delay in the arrival of coastal boats with foodstuffs. Once the boats arrived the problem of malnutrition was largely solved, and with some tuition in various way of cooking things got easier as time passed. And I still have never seen a case of rickets here, in spite of all. Rickets is a childhood bone disorder in which bones soften and become prone to fractures and deformity. The majority of cases occur in children suffering from malnutrition.

Midwifery was my favourite job. It still is. What a comfort to be able to help those women who had suffered with untrained help. The local midwives were so good. They would spend weeks with families, taking care of things, until the mother could get on her feet again. Alas, if they had only been trained they would have been able to avert so much subsequent misery. But even though ante-natal care was unknown and the women who attended childbirth had no training of any kind, they helped to the best of their ability and I was surprised to find so few disasters in their records

After I began to understand my territory I tried to arrange that some pregnant women would get together in Daniel's Harbour where I could see to several cases at one time, in the event they decided to call upon me simultaneously. I have also taken cases into my own home in order to have them on the spot, especially where I suspected some deviation from the normal. My husband has had act to act as anesthetist in some of the more difficult cases.

The one thing I always did insist upon was that babies were breastfed. None of my babies had bottles and I am happy to report that I have never had an outbreak of gastro-enteritis in my years here. Bad mouths and sore bottoms were a rarity too, and quickly disappeared after the mother had advice upon causes etc.

There were some nasty emergencies, of course, and my home became a sort of receiving station as traveling was very difficult because there were no roads and the sea was not always reliable.

I remember one woman we had on a stretcher, on the beach, in quite serious condition, while we waited for the steamer to reach us. By this time, there was a small hospital in Corner Brook to which we hoped to get her. But it was too rough for the steamer to call, so it passed by and we had to convey the woman back to her house. Happily, she survived.

On another occasion, I had a desperately sick woman and there was no steamer due for several days. But we spotted a ship passing and hurriedly launched a boat and put the patient in it. We hailed the ship and requested the crew take the woman to the hospital. Unhappily, this patient had severe kidney damage and did not survive.

In my early years, it was sad to see so many people whose eyesight was poor, and who could not read in any case. One of my 'tools,' which accompanied me on trips along the shore, from settlement to settlement, was a long novel. I would read the novel to an assembled group who would congregate around the kitchen fire on winter evenings. The women would be knitting socks and mitts, or making and mending skin boots, and how they loved hearing a story read.

There was a lot of humour in those early days. Things were not always cold and stormy. There were days when just to walk the miles over the marshes – where marshberries, bakeapples and partridge berries grow, with the sun shining and the sea a smooth sheet of blue – that life was just wonderful.

And funny things happened.

For instance, the one thing I insisted upon was privacy when dealing with any condition. It was, however, customary for neighbours, young and old, to gather around for any, or no, reason whatever. The sight of the nurse going to any house always brought a crowd in to see what was going on. My job then was to ask each individual if they had come for anything, and upon hearing they had not to ask them to leave, unless of course there was a place where I could speak to the patient in privacy.

On one occasion, I remember I went into a house and found the kitchen occupied by the patient, who was sitting in a chair on one side of the stove, with his wife in a chair on the other side, and the whole area on each side filled with neighbours, all squatting around, waiting to hear the diagnosis. They were all adults, so instead of behaving in my usual manner and asking them to leave I joined the crowd, chatting brightly for a minutes. Then, deciding I had better go about my own business, I bid all good night and left.

There was some consternation that I had not proceeded to ask the patient for symptoms but, as I pointed out, my questions were of such a private nature that I did not like to embarrass the man by asking in public. And, seeing him sitting surrounded by friends, I would not ask him to leave them, as apparently he was well enough to have them all there.

These little behaviour patterns of mine had the effect of producing the conditions under which I liked to work. It was surprising that nobody felt any resentment, but acquiesced readily to suggestions I made.

The hospitality offered by everyone with whom I came into contact never ceased to amaze me. At whatever time of day or night I arrived at a home, whether expected or not, I was always offered the best the house had.

Chapter 10

The Baby in the Barn

One's own personal requirements are sometimes ignored when patients are in distress. On one occasion in particular, I had decided that I would be unable to go any distance away for awhile because I was awaiting the birth of one of my own children and it was necessary for me to go by coastal boat to where I myself could get attention.

But as usual a call came and off I went in a boat to a woman who was dying. The poor soul had moved from a different settlement, and the only accommodation obtainable was in a disused barn. It was a barn but I have yet to see a cleaner place in which to live. The floor was scrubbed milk-white and the bedclothes were as clean as water could make them. This in spite of poverty and illness. That woman had managed to make comfortable a place in which to stay under the most difficult of circumstances.

Here in the barn her baby had been born and died and she herself only lived a short time longer. I heard subsequently that the mother had prepared the little body for burial, that the father had made the small coffin and interred the body. So my journey was almost useless apart from giving some comfort to the mother and assuring a more peaceful end. The eldest daughters had been taken in hand by members of the Grenfell Association and had found situations as domestics in United States.

* * * *

My return trip in boat was not so good. The weather had turned stormy and cold and before we reached home, we had to run for shelter in a small settlement about eight miles from Daniel's Harbour. Here I was taken in hand by the grandmother of the place, who put me to bed, and brought hot drinks and food, and insisted upon a thorough rest.

I was not in good condition. After all, tossing around in a small boat in cold wet weather is not the most comfortable way to travel while you are pregnant. However, after a day, due to the kindness of Mrs. Hipsey House, I was fit to resume my journey home.

A young woman there, Mrs. House's daughter-in-law, was also awaiting her first baby. As I could not promise to go back, we decided that the best thing would be for her to accompany me home, which she did. Fortunately, her baby came in good time and in spite of having to share my bed all went well and she was able to return to her home with the new baby.

Mrs. Hipsey House was the midwife and general nurse for all and sundry. She had delivered many babies, and although she had never had any training, she was well experienced and very kind. Her home was the place where travelers stopped, always sure of a welcome and a good meal regardless of station or religion. How many times I have been storm-bound and taken in at that house, and have been treated with such courtesy and attention.

Arriving cold and wet and tired, I have been given the warm slippers right off their own feet while my wet socks were dried and heated, ready for me to resume the journey. Some long cold dark nights in winter, a few women would come in with their knitting and I would read to them. There were no radios, no telephones, no cars, no roads. You went by foot, or horse, or by dogs and whichever way you went, you were exposed to the elements. Sometimes the trips were lovely with bright sun twinkling on the snow-covered trees. Sometimes, you would huddle face down on the sleigh to keep the snow from cutting into your face as it blew. In summer, the boat trips were a joy, until calls came when it was stormy.

Chapter 11

Fried Rabbit, Halibut and Stew

Among the many meals I have eaten at various homes, some stand out particularly. One such was at the home of Mrs. Hipsey House. I arrived at a time when the dinner had been cleared away and supper was not prepared.

Hearing I had not eaten for some time, she immediately brought out a rabbit, caught recently. She pulled off the skin in record time, put it into a hot bake pot with some cut up pork and in less time than it takes to tell, I was enjoying the fried rabbit and it was delicious. When one considers that no money was ever accepted and indeed not offered for such services, you may imagine what kind of hospitality was the rule of this coast.

Another meal that stands out in my mind was that at a home where I had just brought along a baby to a very large family. Of course it was necessary for me to live with the family on these occasions, because it was impossible to do visiting calls with such distances and lack of transportation.

So on this occasion the father of the family asked me what I would like to eat and when I said, "Whatever you have for yourself," he said, "Do you like halibut fins?"

"Well, I have never eaten them, but I will try anything once," I said, so fins it was.

I have never eaten anything I enjoyed so much, either before or since. It was not a matter of hunger being the best sauce. The halibut fins are taken from a large halibut, sliced off the length of the fish, and about five or six inches in depth. These are cleaned, salted, hung to dry, then roasted. The external bony fins are cut away, and only the meaty, oily section is eaten and it is absolutely delicious.

Mrs William Isaac Payne of Parsons Pond was another excellent hostess. Upon arrival there, without any hesitation, one's mitts would be taken and put to dry and warm. The skin boots would be pulled off and slippers supplied, and if the socks were damp, they too would be removed and warm socks provided. As soon as one thawed out, a hot meal would be ready. I have seen this dear soul, having her children around the table ready to eat, seeing a party of travelers arriving, shoo her children off, put the travelers to the same places, letting the children wait until the visitors had eaten because "the strangers are hungrier than you are." As there was always plenty of food the children did not have to go short, but merely had to wait. They never objected – it was part of their lives to help others – and conditions along this coast were such that everyone depended upon such kindness for their very existence. With no commercial place where one could buy a meal, nor hire a bed, it would be unthinkable to let anyone go without such help, and everyone was ready to "go the extra mile" to help.

I remember on one occasion I was attending a maternity case some miles away from home. It was a first baby, and did not seem in any particular hurry to arrive. All was normal, but we could not retire and rest while the patient was experiencing discomfort – so we got to work. The mother-in-law of the patient with whom the young couple still lived had had a large family, and several of the offspring were still of school age and it was spinning and knitting time.

The father-in-law was a fisherman who needed new mitts, so out came the bag of wool. It was in the rough stage, that is, it had been shorn from the sheep, washed, and teased out. The mother-in-law carded with two wooden 'cards' – wooden hand-size slabs with wire hooks covering one side of each. These are pulled against each other over a portion of the rough wool, tearing the fibers straight and forming a roll of more or less straight fibers. These rolls were then passed to me, and I would spin them into yarn with the small foot-propelled spinning wheel. As soon as the yarn was ready, one of the younger girls commenced to knit the mitts, and during the night new mitts were completed for use by father-in-law.

In between the spinning and completion of the mitts, I had set to cook a large pot of stew. We prepared four fresh rabbits, some salt beef, all the vegetables obtainable, potatoes, carrots, turnips and onions with rice as an additive, all cooked together to a degree of tenderness. It was just delicious. The patient commenced the more urgent stage of her motherhood well fortified with this meal, and we attended her had a contented but busy night.

Well, the result was that when the sun rose we had a new baby, a well mother, a proud father, relieved grandparents, a pair of new mitts, a well fed set of attendants, and sufficient food to give all the family another meal. Altogether a satisfactory occasion. It is memories like this that take the sting out of other less happy occasions, and experiences like this that help mothers to approach further births with less apprehension.

Large families were usual, but sometimes occasioned embarrassment, such as the time when I was in attendance at the birth of a baby, the last of a long line. The mother had come to Daniel's Harbour to be near me for the confinement. Meanwhile, the eldest son of the family was to be married here too.

Needless to say, the mother commenced to need my services on the day and at the same time the son was to be married. The new baby arrived and I saw all was well, but there was not time to wash the baby so I hurriedly wrapped the child and left it while I went to the bride's home to help her prepare. Returning to the patient and finding all well I again left to go to the church to play for the wedding. At the conclusion, I returned to the baby case. I washed the child and checked on the mother, after which I was free to go to the reception being held by the newly married couple. Quite a day, everything went well, the mother made a good recovery, and life proceeded as usual.

I once stayed in a small place where a new baby was imminent and the family consisted of the parents and two small sons who were quite a handful. The younger could be managed, but the elder one had opinions of his own. When the baby had arrived and all had gone well and I could spend more time with the two boys one would willingly come to be washed with the baby's nice soap, while the other would have no truck with soap and water, unless the latter required to be the sea near at hand or a forbidden stream. One day, when he was particularly exasperating, I put him in the corner where a stairway led to the upper floor. He was so unusually quiet I congratulated myself that at last he had seen reason. How mistaken I was! When I investigated he was absorbed in a new job – that of taking his father's rifle to pieces. The mother likely had plenty to do when my help was gone and the two lads reverted to the pre-nurse behaviour, although I was assured they were better than they had been and could still be 'controlled' by the reading of a story.

Chapter 12

Appendix Trouble

For the first twenty-one years I spent in Daniel's Harbour I did not see one case of appendicitis. Then a cottage hospital was built at Norris Point, Bonne Bay, about sixty miles away, and it seemed as if it had provoked attacks of appendix trouble. The first one was quite an acute one and as it occurred in April was very difficult to get to the hospital, because the marshes, rivers and ponds in our route were in the process of opening. Nothing on wheels could get over it, and dogs could not pull a komatik over it, the sea was not open so a boat could not be considered. The only thing was for the men to do something about it. They did. Several of them took ropes, got the patient secured upon a komatik as warm and comfortable as possible under the circumstances, put the ropes attached to the komatik over their shoulders and pulled the patient the sixty miles to hospital. An appendectomy was performed, the first in my experience here. The patient remained in hospital until she was recovered enough to return to her home. The men of course came back as soon as they had seen the patient looked after by the hospital staff. This journey was not for payment. The men volunteered and were well rewarded in the knowledge they had been able to help and that they were instrumental in saving the life of a woman. I have often wondered what would have happened if these fine men had not been concerned enough to want to help in this case of need.

Chapter 13

Winter

Winter in Newfoundland is a lovely season. The long light days with myriads of sparkling reflections from frosty layers of snow, and the beautiful sculptures formed by wind eddying around snowdrifts give one a feeling of beauty that can only be realized by actual experience.

To drive through a narrow path seated on a komatik, pulled by a team of dogs running silently, the trees meeting overhead and weighed with snow, one appears to be going on an endless journey through a fairylike tunnel.

Upon emerging into a clearing where the brilliant sun shines down upon the virgin whiteness, the air warm and still, it is a joy to stay a short while and drink in the beauty of it all. A shrill piping of a small bird or the scurrying of a rabbit across the path, might interrupt the stillness, but the beauty is still there.

There are other times when the snow, in spite of its beauty, becomes a handicap, and one such occasion became impressed upon my memory by events occurring after a particularly severe storm, when snow drifted to high dimensions, and a call came from an isolated logging camp.

This was one of the most distressing cases I remember

and it was to do with a woman who had gone to live in a lumber camp with her husband for the winter months.

She reckoned to be able to get home in time for the expected baby to arrive some months later. Unfortunately, she became ill and the husband had to come out from the camp to get help.

He telephoned me from the next settlement where a post office telephone was connected with one here at the post office. My husband and I set forth immediately with our horse and sleigh, but after plunging through deep snow for a couple of miles we came to a snowdrift about twenty feet high. We tried all ways to get over but it proved an insuperable barrier and we had to retreat with the horse quite exhausted from the efforts we had made.

Before daylight next morning the husband arrived here on foot. He had come to meet us, had encountered the huge snowdrift on the other side, had taken his horse out of the shafts of the sleigh, led it into a tiny clearing among some trees where he tied it, put down some hay, covered it with a blanket and left it for the night, while he tramped up and down and over the drift with snowshoes, making a sort of path over which we could proceed with snowshoes, but over which no beast could go. Once more we left with our horse, reached the drift, and climbed over it. My husband returned home with the horse and the patient's husband harnessed his horse and we eventually reached the camp where we were anxiously awaited.

I found the patient had been delivered of one baby a few days previously and a second one a few days later. The delivery was not finally completed, and the patient had suffered blood loss to a dangerous degree. There were few facilities for dealing with such a case but all possible under the circumstances was done and the patient made a good recovery. Neither of the twins survived, one factor being the prematurity, another was the RH blood factor, and yet another was the lack of skilled help. The camp was very cold as the winter was extreme and there was not sufficient warmth for the occupancy of any but the most robust.

All these things were accepted with the recognized fatalistic feeling that no other way of life was possible and it has taken many years of teaching to bring home the knowledge that life held more than just working and eating, and accepting misfortunes.

Only a couple of days ago, many years after I had 'resigned,' I was called upon for help with an emergency maternity patient. But this time things were indeed different. Now, we have a road and in spite of one of the heaviest falls of snow and consequent drifts, the plow went ahead while my son and I conveyed the patient to hospital in a warm car.

There she will have all the necessary attention, a skilled doctor, well trained nurses, and a great relief on the part of friends and relations that she does not have to accept just what one pair of hands can do, in indifferent surroundings.

Usually my return from a couple of days away meant a back log of calls had piled up. As I have previously said, the only telephones existing in those days linked up the post offices along the coast, so that during the hours when the post offices were closed, and during holidays, there was no way to get a call through, however urgent the need. Therefore, if my services were required at such times, a friend or relative of the sick person would have to come along to tell me. If the patient could be brought along, that was sometimes done too, but because of lack of knowledge concerning the severity of the illness, or otherwise, sometimes some of the calls and visits were not really necessary.

I remember one call which of course happened on a particularly vicious day in winter. A garbled message reached me that a women needed me: "She had her baby but now she's in racks of pain and we think something has been left behind."

The woman lived a long way away, and with my heart in my boots I started off. I had had a strenuous week and was extremely tired. However, thinking the condition could be very serious, I feared to delay and take a rest. The snow continued to fall, and it became impossible to make much speed in such depth of soft snow; the horse could only flounder along in spurts, and of course trying to get along on foot was out of the question.

For hours, Angus and I plodded on, eventually reaching a settlement where we were persuaded to stay and rest up the horse. After the very welcome cup of tea, we rested awhile, only to be called at twelve midnight by the relatives of the patient who had become alarmed at our non-arrival and feared we had met with trouble.

Feeling still more tired and miserable and cold, off we all went again on the weary drag through the dark – the shadowy figures of the men swaying with lighted lanterns ahead, stamping a pathway for the horse that was to follow. Huge snowflakes continued to fall, muffling sounds, so that it became a weird dream that seemed to be endless. Finally we saw lights ahead and willing hands came to help us into the house and stable for the poor horse, who had indeed earned a rest.

The kitchen was bright and warm, a sharp contrast from the dark and cold outside. I felt overcome. My face was so stiff with the cold that I could not speak, my hands were helpless.

Soon women were helping me to remove my snow covered clothing, shaking off the snow, pulling of my skin boots, and trying to make me as comfortable as they could.

My frozen mitts were put to thaw, and I sat on the floor by the stove with my feet underneath the stove, just absorbing heat.

Because of the intense cold I had endured my mind was incapable of much activity. The tiredness I had when I started on the trip and the misery endured on the way acted as a sort of anesthetic and for some minutes I could only sit near the heat, and try to flex my fingers and toes. After more hot tea it was not too long before I was able to speak, and I asked to see the patient.

I went into the bedroom to see if I could find out what the condition was, and if I could do anything for the woman. But my brain refused to function. I could not think. So, in case I would make some mistake in diagnosis, I gave the patient two Aspirin tablets to ease her pain and suggested that we rest awhile until I had returned to normal and would then examine her.

I told the attendants to lie down and sleep, and now I stretched myself out on a settle in the warm kitchen and fell into a deep sleep. Upon awakening some hours later, I found somebody had quietly kept the fire replenished all night and that everyone else was refreshed by a rest.

After a cup of hot tea I went in to examine the patient again only to find her apparently quite well. All her pain had gone, she had slept well, and I could not find anything the matter with her. She said the 'pills' had cured her and there was nothing to worry about.

I found that the baby was not as new as I had supposed, but nearly six weeks old. What had caused the worry over the mother's condition I could not ascertain, merely that she had not been well since the baby arrived.

Of course, it was a relief that there was nothing needing attention, but when I think of the men and horses who had undergone so much distress to get me there it seemed a pity.

* * * *

The sequel to this adventure was surprising. I was credited with being clever enough to diagnose on sight and to give the right medicine immediately with the result that the cure was so rapid. The woman was immediately up and about doing her chores as usual.

It was rather a good thing to have had this reputation, because it inspired confidence in many who had shirked coming for treatment, preferring to rely upon home cures and superstitious methods of dealing with ills and accidents.

The real truth I could not of course disclose, and I basked in this undeserved glory for a long time. But just in case I was still numb and had overlooked anything, I stayed around and saw a few other patients in the village. After a while, when I saw that the woman was really well, I returned to my home. This time the snow had ceased falling, the sun was shining making the return journey a delight; so different from the night trip with an anxious mind.

Chapter 14

Hallelujah!

On one occasion I had been attending cases in the settlement of Port au Choix. As the visits had been completed I prepared to return along the coast to my headquarters. Just then a boat came in, bringing a family: husband, wife and a small girl. The child was emaciated and very weak, eleven months old. I decided to accompany the family to their home, where I hoped to be able to do something for the child, who weighed around eleven pounds.

The story was sad. Just two weeks earlier the mother had given birth to another child who had died. The mother was in poor condition herself, but the loss of the new baby and the feebleness of the older child had spurred her into making the journey for help. I accompanied the family to their home by boat.

I wished to prepare a feed for the hungry child but I was assured that she would not swallow milk. In my ignorance, I decided they had a problem of not preparing it properly so I proceeded with the preparation. I found the parents were right; the child would not suck the milk from the bottle.

As I watched the parents prepare another feed I could understand the reason for the child's sad condition. They had no idea about infant feeding at all. They fed the child a bottle which I saw being filled with strong tea, some molasses added for sweetening, and cold cocoa to cool it down. To add to my amazement, the nipple on the bottle was then sucked by an adult who had nasty looking teeth. The idea was to try the warmth of the concoction and start the flow. The nipple had been torn and sewn up again with white thread but a large knot had been left on the tip which had the effect of scouring the hard palate when the child sucked. That accounted for the nasty sore I observed on the child's palate.

And so my initiation continued. But when an older member of the family took the child up and, after dipping bread into pea soup, proceeded to suck the bread dry then place it into the child's mouth, I decided it would be better to have the child completely in my own care. Therefore, we set off again in boat for the remaining twenty or so miles to Daniel's Harbour.

Arriving there, my treatment commenced with graduated hot baths, body and limb rubbing with oil, wrapping in cotton wool, wrapping around with flannel bandages, so providing regular warmth to the little shriveled limbs. Now came the fight. The baby had to drink milk, so with a new and sterilized bottle and nipple, I prepared the feed, adding to it some Vitrol, which was considered such a help in cases of malnutrition. Holding the cocoon-like bundle in my arms, I put the bottle to the baby's mouth.

With an angry gesture, the child jerked its head away, closing the mouth against the nipple. Gently opening the mouth, I pushed the nipple in again, meanwhile walking around, and crooning to the child, hoping to distract its attention and get it to at least taste the feed. Nothing doing.

The child cried and as soon as it opened its mouth to cry I squirted some milk in and tilted the child to compel it to swallow. This maneuver continued for about thirty or more minutes, during which I made the child swallow four ounces of milk, and at the end of that time, both the child and I were exhausted.

The child, now warm, fed and very tired, went to sleep, and the mother and I rejoiced at this victory. Daily this treatment was repeated at two long intervals until at least the child accepted the feed without fuss. Daily graduated hot baths were given, and it was a joyful moment when I was able to show the mother that the child was gaining weight, its mouth was nicely healed, and the skin assumed a healthy pink appearance, that vomiting had ceased, and normal functions restored.

The weekly weighings of the child were anxiously watched by neighbours, all of whom had been concerned about the possible failure of my ministrations, but who rejoiced wholeheartedly at its success. After a few weeks, I considered that the mother could now return to her home with the baby, knowing how to attend to its needs. Of course by then, the wool wrapping had been removed and normal clothing replaced so the only thing for the mother to do was to attend tho the food problem, and I know she learned that lesson well, because the next time I saw that child, she was a lovely healthy well developed girl.

* * * *

Quite a different case was that of a woman in Cow Head, nearly 30 miles south, who had been delivered of her first child, had convulsions, and had lapsed into a coma. Two days later, I was sent for. It was such a stormy day that a large skiff was used for the sea trip. I didn't know it at the time but the man who had been requested to come for me earlier had not left his home because, he said, for one thing it was too rough and for another the woman would be dead before I got there. At midday, when it was reckoned I should be arriving and people had gathered at the shore to see my arrival, they realized that the boat had not left to bring me. Six men immediately launched a skiff and sailed through the storm to get me. When I left Daniel's Harbour with them my landlady stood weeping because she was sure I would never be seen again. I had only been in Daniel's Harbour for six weeks at this point.

Arriving late at night, I found the patient quite unconscious, her whole body grossly bloated, her tongue bitten, her lips and face so swollen as to make her unrecognizable. It would be difficult to describe my feelings as I saw her condition. She really needed hospital care. How I longed for transportation, for a hospital, for a doctor, for another nurse.

But there was no time for wishful thinking. I picked up a stick of wood from the pile behind the stove, wrapped it in cloth, and put it between the woman's teeth to save further laceration of the tongue so badly bitten during convulsions. Then the organization of friends to help. How good they were.

The minister had been sent for and the valiant Reverend Greavett became my child helper. The men kept the wood supply chopped and fed into the stove in order to get a constant supply of hot water. The women filled everything capable of holding water from the outside well and passed it to the indoor women who heated it and passed it to me. Everything heatable was used, plates, hot water bags, pan lids, flat irons, anything which could hold heat was packed around the patient to induce perspiration.

Revered Greavett and I took turns in the constant irrigation of the tissues. He stood on a chair, holding up a container from which a tube conveyed the solution to the patient while I was at the bedside directing the flow, and receiving the contaminated water. This, in turn, was passed out to another of the team, who took it away to a suitable place for discard.

The bedroom was just behind the kitchen, an ideal situation for the purpose, being near our helpers and warm from the stove. Before long, Reverend Greavett was compelled to remove his collar, then his coat. But he never faltered in the administration – stoop, dip, pour into the container, stoop, dip, pour into the container. We would occasionally change places and I would stoop, dip and pour. It seemed endless, no sound but what we made with the gurgling water and the stertorous breathing of the unconscious woman on the bed.

The pulse rate was unaccountable. It was like a tight string, but as the skin began to get moist with perspiration the pulse rate could be distinguished. At first count, it was around 180. We continued unceasingly for 24 hours, not stopping for rest or food, and when we saw a profuse sweat appear we could have cheered. So the night and day passed with everyone working to capacity in that small house.

By the next evening we knew we had won. The pulse rate had come down to 80, the skin was moist and shrinking, the mouth was better, the breathing less harsh, the eyes could be seen to open. We were so overjoyed we could have shouted hallelujah.

But we were almost too tired to rejoice, and with thanks to God for sparing this life we decided to rest a while. In spite of having worked as hard as we had done our helpers insisted on letting me rest while they stood guard. So I went into a corner where, upon the nice clean floor with my head on a pillow, I slept soundly. The helpers crept around, keeping the fire fed and preparing a meal for after the rest.

A day later I was able to return to my headquarters knowing the patient would go on to complete recovery. I was so glad to have been able to render assistance when it was so direly needed. The woman recovered to live a normal life and produced a large healthy family.

Chapter 15

Training Midwives

I had heard of cases where mothers had apparently delivered normally but had subsequently died. It was reckoned that as the breast milk not made its appearance, that act had been the cause of the death. It is of course one of the symptoms of septicemia that no milk comes. That is one of the signs of infection, and not one of the causes of death.

I had also seen cases of women who had literally bled white as the result of ignorance, carelessness or mishandling of them during parturition. I have arrived at cases to be greeted by a smiling attendant who would assure me that 'everything was over,' only to find on approaching the bed that indeed it nearly was all over. True, the child had been born, but the mother's condition called for immediate and skilled help. A little further delay in getting help to her would have resulted in yet another death. The attendant may not have realized the condition; it was not unkindness but ignorance. The patient on the one hand, not liking to 'make a fuss,' and the attendant not knowing enough to understand the woman's life blood was quietly oozing away. To them, having got the baby into the world was all that mattered.

There have been cases where the birth was not completed and retained matter set up infection with fatal results. I remember the case of a young woman who died of septicemia while I was seriously ill with pneumonia. Part of the afterbirth had been retained and the result was a deadly infection. The older lady who had delivered her went on to deliver another woman within a few days and the second patient became seriously ill. In this case the woman did survive but was unable to attend to her household duties for almost a year afterwards.

All of these things helped me to decide to try to train suitable young women in midwifery, so that in the event of need during my absence with other cases, or in case of illness on my part, there would be reliable help. This of course was before the antibiotic era. But these pupils did learn the meaning of sepsis and its prevention, and their hands became well scrubbed every time they attended cases, even if they did not manipulate the patient at all.

To begin with, six women applied for training and they agreed to come to my home for lectures, and to accompany me to cases for practical instruction. This venture proved very worthwhile and the students made excellent practical nurses. They learned to understand the difference between the normal and the abnormal, and when they became capable of conducting deliveries on their own, would realize and report to me any sign of symptoms which deviate in the slightest from the normal, and so enable me to get to the scene of operations before too long a time had elapsed from their observation and the onset of treatment. I myself know personally of lives which would have been lost but for their good work and conscientious behaviour.

One old lady who had been practicing for a number of years was illiterate, and so could not benefit much from lectures. She had had no training of any kind, but she was kindness itself. She would stay by a patient for hours, and after the delivery, would gather up the soiled linen and take it home to wash. She would prepare meals for the family and pay daily visits for ten days attending to mother and child. For all this, she would not accept any payment.

Because of her lifetime of work, and with the first hand experience she had had, I considered that what I could teach her would be very little. There was so much dignity about the old lady that I could not suggest that she come to me to learn. After all, she was getting too old to be able to carry on many more years, and my trained women would be at her elbow in need and they would be able to take over when she had to quit.

This lady's home was my headquarters when I was in that district and she looked after me as well as a mother would have done. At night when I was there, after the day's work was done, she would prepare work of some kind that she could do by lamplight. A few neighbours would come in, and we would gather around her kitchen table, the kerosene lamp shedding a soft light, and I would read aloud from one of the books which I usually took along when leaving home for any length of time.

The women were so glad; it opened a new world for them to hear a tale of some far off place, or of adventure. Many were the pleasant nights so spent with neighbours who heard of these readings and would make a point of coming in, bringing their ever present knitting or boot-making or repairing.

All their cares dropped away while they lived in the atmosphere of the story, and occasionally I would notice a tear being furtively wiped away at some pathetic incident in the story, as during the reading of some of Dickens. Now these people have passed onto their reward which I am sure must be heaven for they did indeed care for the stranger, feed the hungry, and comfort the sick.

As my class of midwives progressed in their studies, sometimes weather would prevent their attendance at my home for lectures, so I would take along the lesson when visiting other places and arrange a session with whatever pupil lived at that particular place. Two pupils at a time would accompany me to gain practical experience, and eventually deliver a baby under my supervision. They took a rather intensified course for six months before being allowed to actually undertake a case, and then only when I was completely satisfied that all ante-natal care had been given, and as far as it was possible to estimate that the case would be quite normal.

During the training period of these midwives, a case occurred where an untrained woman had delivered a mother and caused a condition needing surgery. The untrained midwife did not recognize the injury and the patient became infected.

A few days after the delivery, one of my trainees heard about the patient and called upon her. Realizing what was wrong, she immediately telegraphed me and I went along forthwith.

By now I had antibiotics to work with and I was very thankful for them when I found the condition the mother was in. I stayed by for a few days and finally the infection was overcome and she went on to complete recovery.

Later on she was operated on and the surgical repairs done, and she has since had other children with no ill effects. It may be imagined how very thankful I was that my training of the woman who alerted me to the problem had been so fruitful.

So many similar cases were averted by these midwives' vigilance and now one never hears of puerperal sepsis. The trainees have scattered now but I hear of the good work they still do.

The trained midwives proved a very valuable addition to the health service and here I would like to point out that breast feeding of the newly born was mandatory, excepting in cases of TB or heart trouble. I believe my success in having no cases of gastro-enteritis in babies was because I insisted on breast feeding.

The custom then was that any mother who had a baby breast feeding would also feed the newly born child until its own mother's milk became available, say in a couple of days. The first time I saw this being done I really said some things, pointing out the unsuitability of the milk for the newborn who should have been getting colostrum from its own mother. As TB was prevalent at that time I used that as an argument against the practice and really put my foot down.

Chapter 16

A Man of Vision

For the first two years of my service in Daniel's Harbour I received $900 per annum, or $75 a month, which was a small fortune to people who received very little return for their services, or fish caught and cured, or pelts of foxes and beavers. But, alas, the very generous people of St. John's who had supported this venture could not continue so my salary ceased.

The terms of my engagement clearly stated that I was to receive $1,000 per annum. After I had received a number of cheques for $75 a month I politely told Lady Harris this would not add up to the correct total of $1,000 by the end of the year. She said simply that while no one was trying to cheat me there just wasn't the money to pay me what I had been promised.

After my term with NONA had expired no nurse was sent to replace me. The next available nurse being stationed thirty miles north and separated from us by streams, ponds and a bay the result was that patients who could reach the other nurse continued to call for my services, so I was compelled to continue as usual, but with no salary, no authority to refer patients to hospital, no drugs other than those I could buy and pay for myself, I was really on my own.

This condition lasted for another ten years, during which time patients were hospitalized in my home, minor surgery performed on my kitchen table and childbirth conducted in the homes of the patients, and occasionally in my own home, when it was necessary for me to keep a patient under observation before delivery. Patients still came from other places for help, because the other nurse was a day's journey away by sea and weather was not always suitable for small boats to trust to a day's journey, especially with a sick person aboard. Fees charged, but seldom collected, were fifty cents for a nursing call and $5 for a delivery. A tooth extraction was fifty cents.

Even when traveling by coastal boat, I would take along tooth forceps and a few dressings and medicines in case of emergency. Sometimes a crew member would be glad to have a tooth extracted instead of having to wait out the time until he could return to St. John's to see a dentist. No anesthetic would be used, but that did not deter the sufferer from getting the offended molar removed and how grateful he was to be free of pain.

As a reward for this ten years of voluntary service, I was awarded the Medal of the British Empire, but 25 years had elapsed before this came to pass and conditions were almost as bad as when I had first arrived, because now we were caught up in the hungry thirties.

Improvements in general had been accomplished: knowledge of preventive medicine was beginning to trickle through and people came in the early stages of illness instead of delaying too long to get a chance of a cure. Accidents presented themselves as soon as possible after the mishap, and mouths were in better condition. But the dreadful poverty, as well as the isolation, made it difficult to promote the health standard which was of course the ultimate aim.

Governor Gordon MacDonald was to decorate me with the medal and he arrived by frigate at Port Saunders where the investiture was to take place in the summer of 1946. I proceeded by the local small steamer and duly received the medal which was awarded for "25 years of devoted service."

This opportunity to emphasize our needs for better communications could not be missed, so the matter was discussed. If we had any glimmer of hope before then, it was certainly extinguished.

The reply to our request for a road was "Absolutely not." Governor MacDonald went on to say, "There is no possible chance of building a road along this coast where so few people live." So that was that.

Nevertheless, we continued agitating and writing to the powers-that-be, hoping against hope we might finally wear them down and eventually get a road of sorts, by which we could get any very sick person to hospital without having to depend on wind and weather for their transportation.

* * * *

Nobody had thought in the days of such poverty and depression that there would come a man to serve his country with dedication and fearless vision, the final result of which was to help raise the standard of living, provide us with the road we had so long agitated for, and improved health services. In 1949, just 28 years after I arrived here, Joseph Smallwood became the leader of this small country.

A man of vision, with unbounded energy, he gave and gives of his best to the uplifting and improvement of the island. His chosen few, with whom he made up his cabinet, have given him absolute loyalty, and their combined efforts in each of their posts has resulted in such a civil revolution that only those of us who experienced the hardships of the early harder years can appreciate to the full what has been done, and is still being done by this dynamic leader.

Under Mr. Smallwood's guidance, Newfoundland became a province of Canada, and immediately benefited by the social security program of Canada. Family allowances were received, and almost overnight the improvement was apparent in the dress and feeding habits of the families.

Only those of us who have experienced the hardships and inconvenience and heartbreak of the pre-Confederation days can realize what a complete revolution has taken place – a revolution that would have been unthinkable twenty years ago.

I suppose every age produces its outstanding leader, and we in Newfoundland are indeed lucky that our strong man is one whose dedication to Newfoundland and its welfare is so great.

So many leaders have only their own prestige in view, and it is refreshing to find one so selfless, as to sacrifice his own comfort and well being to serve the province as the leader we have today. That he has been ably and well supported by his Cabinet members goes without saying, and I would like to pay a personal tribute to each one of them.

Today, just fifteen years after we were assured that no road would ever be made along the coast, we are enjoying a road that extends the whole length of the coast, and will before too long encircle the island.

To attempt to record significant changes and improvements in the history of a country must of necessity be a stupendous task, but maybe a few notes of changes, especially those which have occurred during one's own life time, and in one's own district, may be of interest or amusement to those who come after us, and who have never endured the trials and tribulations of their predecessors.

* * * *

Forty years ago, in this tight little island, things were extremely backward: lack of communications and roads, completely isolated fishing settlements, the only contact with the outside world the coastal boat which was only able to call in good weather. Only very rough weather prevented this sturdy little steamer from calling at every place on its list. But in Daniel's Harbour there was no harbour in which the steamer could shelter in stormy weather so the passing by of the steamer made life a little harder, when no mail and no freight could be landed.

Then there were the times when I would be returning to my home headquarters and would be unable to get ashore and so would have to go on to another place until the weather abated. During the winter months, mail came overland by teams of various kinds, varying from dogs pulling a komatick to the occasional horse and sleigh, and sometimes an ox pulling a sleigh. It was a leisurely procedure, depending again on the weather. Many nights my kitchen was made "odorous" by dog harnesses, which had to be dried around the stove, the team having to seek shelter from storms, and the mail courier needing rest and food.

Chapter 17

A Visit to England

After seven years in Daniel's Harbour I decided it was time to visit my parents in London and let my two children, nearly five and nearly two, meet their English grandparents, so I arranged as best I could that someone would attend to things while I was away. While I was in England I met a woman named Becky who was homeless and the mother of a child 10 months old. She had been married and her husband deserted her, and her parents were dead. The only outlook for her was life in the poorhouse and her child to be raised in an orphanage. I offered her a home if she cared to come to Newfoundland and she gladly accepted, so my family increased by one adult and one boy. She fell in love with Newfoundland and after several years married a fisherman and left us. Becky and Pat Dwyer settled in St. John's and raised a nice large family who have all done well for themselves.

While I was away, Angus met a lad of 13, who had left his 'guardian' because he had been so badly neglected. He was in a sad condition, ragged and footsore. Upon my arrival home, Angus told me about the lad and his need. Poor lad. He was a bright intelligent boy and sadly in need of a home and some kindness. We brought him to our house, provided a hot bath... my husband cut his hair short and I washed his head in a Lysol solution. Then, having burned his rags in the kitchen stove, I made a suit of underwear from fleecy cotton, pants from some material I had, and put him to bed on the kitchen day bed. He slept soundly, and when my husband was lighting the stove next morning the lad had awakened and started to cry. This alarmed us and my husband asked why the tears. The lad replied, "I thought I was in Heaven."

We were all grieved when he decided to leave us after a time, but happily he became a member of another family and went on to better things. He became well educated and taught school... married and raised a lovely family which includes a doctor, a nurse, and some teachers.

Myra and Nurse Harvey at Cabot Tower in St. John's in 1921

Myra and Angus's marriage certificate

*Myra in
Newfoundland*

*Angus at age 17
in Halifax*

Leaving to go on a case. Myra is behind the driver

Cottage Hospital in Bonne Bay 1953

Tooth extraction in Myra's kitchen in Daniel's Harbour

Myra, Angus and baby Grace in their back garden in Daniel's Harbour

Newfoundland Governor Gordon MacDonald and Myra in 1946

Choir Myra started in Daniel's Harbour. She made the surplices for everyone. The man on the right is John Moss who subsequently became the rector in Gander.

Confirmation. Myra made the girls' dresses and veils

Northern Ranger arriving at Daniel's Harbour

*Angus preparing
fish for dinner*

*Small house on
the left is home of
Angus's parents in
Daniel's Harbour
in 1921*

Angus in 1949

Below:
Mr. and Mrs. George
Moss, the couple Myra
first boarded with in
Daniel's Harbour

Daniel's Harbour in the 1930s

Becky and Pat Dwyer. Becky was an Englishwoman Myra invited to come to Newfoundland. She later married Pat Dwyer and they settled in St. John's

Myra making mats

Myra playing her organ

Myra receiving her Ph.D in 1974

Trevor, son of Myra and Angus, with girlfriend Mildred Field, in 1951. They were married in 1952.

Grace and Barbara daughters of Myra and Angus

Chapter 18

Community Work

In Daniel's Harbour there was only one public building, a one room school which also served as a church. It had a small extension added to provide a sanctuary and was closed off from the school room by a double door. When services were held, the door was opened and the congregation occupied the desks, which had been made in the homes of the pupils.

The minister was unable to visit very frequently because of the long strip of territory he had to cover, so his method was to stay a few days in each place and proceed when weather and opportunity offered. During these visits there would be several services with Holy Communion, all the recent babies would be baptized, perhaps a wedding and of course instruction for confirmation.

Children who attend school and church in the same building, sitting in the same desks for each occasion, will naturally get very little idea of religion, and as the boys would be leaving school at around twelve years of age to go and help in the fishing boats and the girls to enter 'domestic' service, the church did not mean too much to them. The girls would be hired for a week or two, when a baby was expected, and would be paid with a garment or so. Thus the religious instruction consisted of learning the Creed, the ten commandments and the catechism and the fact that Christmas meant a new dress for the girls and new trousers for the lads, if they were lucky.

As soon as I could manage it, I decided to do something about the church. The sanctuary when I first saw it, was cobwebby, stained by a leaky roof, discoloured cloths, dim brass candlesticks. It was a mess! I had to raise funds somehow, but how? A kind friend, Mrs. Aiken from England, sent me some material from which I made screens, dividing the sanctuary from the schoolroom. I removed the big ugly doors, cleaned and varnished the walls and floors, cleaned the accumulation of grease and corrosion from the candlesticks, and debated on how to get new altar coverings.

I got all the school children together, and began to teach them songs and recitations and to put on shows, for which we charged small sums for admission and gradually raised enough to buy some materials, which we sewed and made to cover the altar. Then as time went on, we continued these shows until we had accumulated one hundred dollars with which we bought a small organ.

Prior to that, we had used my organ. I had a secondhand organ which I had bought from a church outside our parish for my own use. It stood in my kitchen where we had our rehearsals and would then be carried on a hand-barrow to the school for the performances. The acquisition of an organ which could remain in the school for church use was quite an accomplishment, and I acted as organist for nearly forty years.

As before I came there was nobody here with any knowledge of music it was a welcome and enjoyable thing for the people of our place to be able to hear and sing with music, and the house used to fill with men each evening after the chores were done. They would sing away with great gusto, all the old fashioned hymns of their childhood, for hours on end.

With the passing of time and the increasing population, a larger school was needed, but still we had the same outfit – the sanctuary attached to the school. However, from small acorns big oaks grow, and today we just completed a large modern church, the first one to be built here. Just one hundred years ago, the first Anglican service was held here by Reverend Rule, an Englishman who traveled the long coast to do whatever he could for the scattered inhabitants.

Today we have the new church, with a robed choir, two servers at the altar, a cross bearer and a regular set of services provided by a young newly ordained minister, who can come and go over a well made road, more or less regardless of weather conditions. We have a well organized and active Church of England Women's Association and an Anglican Young Peoples' Association. These two organizations are of considerable help in the church, and by their efforts we hope to have the last dollar of the debt we incurred in building paid, and we shall have the dedication of our lovely church.

We have a flourishing Home and School Association, which contributes occasionally to our funds. There is indeed a great improvement since 1921. I omitted to say, that the first service conducted here was in the kitchen of a fisherman, there being not even a school then.

Today, we have a new five room school where students are staying to finish Junior Matriculation, and from which there have gone lads and girls to take up various professions. One of our lads is now the rector of one of the largest congregations in Newfoundland. Several girls are registered nurses, many of them are teachers, as well as some of the lads who have taken degrees in college, and are now teaching. But of all the improvements, the most gratifying to me personally is the existence of a church building where children may realize the true meaning of religion with reverence.

Chapter 19

Merry Christmas

I found that most families were foresighted enough to provide for seasons when it would not be possible to secure food. During the fishing season the men would salt away fish, that is codfish and herring, which would also be used for bait in the next fishing season. A quantity of herring would be put down for dog feed too, since dogs were the means of pulling home the firewood as well as transporting travelers. Berries were picked and preserved, and there was nearly always jam available.

Every family owned a cow, so butter, milk and cream were all on the menu. Rabbits provided tasty meals, and deer and moose could be caught. Most families kept some sheep, so wool was home grown, and there would be an occasional mutton for the pot. Vegetables were planted in spring, and usually there were enough reaped to last until planting time again. Then if vegetables had become scarce, the young dock leaves and 'lambs tails' made good healthy additions to the diet.

I learned so much from these outport people. I learned how to shear sheep, make knitted wear right from the sheep's back – including carding, spinning, dyeing, knitting and weaving. I learned how to tan sealskins, and make them into boots and slippers. I learned how to make the warm rugs from strips of rag hooked into burlap, which made the homes so cheerful with the bright hues and patterns. I learned how to cook the Newfoundland food and how to make bread, and above all I learned how to split wood with an axe so that I was never short of fuel or warmth, if I should happen to come to a home where there was nothing ready.

I learned how to sleep with one ear open so that I was almost ready when harness bells came jingling in the night for a call away. Oh yes, many things not taught in training schools must be learned when one goes to live where things are somewhat primitive and isolated.

* * * *

Then of course there was a great deal of pleasure and amusement for you would be hard pressed to find a merrier time than was spent during the twelve days of Christmas. Most homes would have a keg of home brewed beer in readiness and every visitor would be invited to taste it.

And if in some instances the recipient became a bit merry, I think it was not so much the potency of the brew, as the condition of the drinker, who may not have been accustomed to drinking any beer at all, and who possibly had visited several homes on his course to greet his friends and neighbours.

There would be the huge raisin pudding boiling merrily on the stove and an oven-full of good meats sending forth the delicious aroma, that made visitors unhesitatingly accept an invitation to "sit in." Indeed, wherever one found oneself at any mealtime in any place, it was considered the correct thing to share the meal. No formal invitation would be issued, merely a casual "Have you been to dinner?" If this was responded with a shake of the head the response was, "Well, sit right in."

Another place would be prepared at the table, and the visitor, who would be an absolute stranger, maybe just passing through, or a VIP on some official business, or a close relative, it mattered not. The hospitality was unlimited. Each evening for twelve days, commencing on December 23, or Tipsy Eve as it is called, there would be a dance for all comers in somebody's kitchen. The biggest kitchens were of course in demand, and some of us have floors scoured down to the knots by the vigorous dancing of the lads and lasses – and indeed of the staider folks too – as a memento of the far off days before the introduction of radio and other diversions.

There would be a local fiddler who would be excellent at keeping time and playing the appropriate tunes. He had to be a good tempered fellow; he never received payment – but would play for hours on end, until almost daylight.

After the twelve days of Christmas had passed, everyone settled away again to their usual occupations. Some men went into the woods to cut the year's firewood, others to trap for fur, some to snare rabbits. The children returned to the one room school, the mothers to the usual chores of housekeeping, spinning, and mat-hooking.

In every home one would see the mat frame erected, one or more of the womenfolk working at the new mat, perhaps a neighbour helping, and enjoying a chat. The spinning wheel was a permanent part of the furniture, and the girls would practice spinning at intervals, but the mother would be the chief adviser and spinner. Knitting needles and yarn were always in evidence and the smallest girls would have a sock or mitt 'in the knit' at all times.

Chapter 20

TB a challenge
but life not all work

Tuberculosis became one of my biggest challenges. It took a lot of preaching to convince people that it was both contagious and curable. The very fact that relatives who had lived with and nursed people in their final days with the disease and yet themselves had not succumbed seemed proof positive that TB was not catching. People thought it was cruel to isolate a patient with TB, and instead would sit by the bedside to keep the sufferer company. The sickroom became a meeting place because the friends could not bear to think of the patient being alone. I would lecture, describe, warn, appeal, but to little avail. I was considered to be 'TB' mad.

What a difference today. With the opening of the sanatorium at Corner Brook in 1950 and frequent X-rays, with antibiotics, and the resultant education, people have realized what can be done, and I like to feel I was instrumental in laying the foundation stone of the movement.

Now we enjoy the highroad. Now we can get suspicious cases along right away for diagnosis and treatment. Now we have people willing and anxious to take treatment. The veil of secrecy and ignorance has been lifted, and such words as inoculation, pneunothorax, penicillin, streptomycin, in common use, and what is more, intelligent use. When patients need to have repeated injections of some of the drugs, they will come to some of us who, although not now actively engaged in nursing, can still administer treatment, thus saving the patient the long journey to hospital, but also helping to lighten the outpatient load of the hospitals.

* * * *

Life here was not all work and emergencies. There were the long hot days when we would help to make hay, and pick gallons of fresh wild raspberries in between turning the hay to eat later with plenty of our home produced cream. There were the cool fall days when gallons of marsh berries would be picked on the marshes providing the most delicious jam. Blueberries grew profusely and when cloud berries (bakeapples) were ripe everyone picked as many as they could carry home. These made a source of income, because people would pack them in one-pound tins, and they would find a ready sale for them. Even in these days of greater prosperity, people still pick and sell these berries.

There are few cows kept today. Prosperity has rather spoilt the idea of providing ones own provender. For one thing with children attending school until their teens, there is not the labour force available. At one time children would stay home from school to help do planting and reaping, to go for the cow, to help catch fish. But now, they are trying to get an education, and cannot lose school days for any reason but illness. So the parents must accommodate their lives to this new tempo. It is easier to buy a tin of milk than to keep a cow, although not so nice, and vegetables may be bought instead of having to spend so many days growing them oneself. Then there are other diversions now, at one time work was the only diversion. There were no radios, books were scarce, and readability was still more scarce, so its not to be wondered at that people readily turned to amusements after years of nothing but toil, with little reward.

I remember when my radio was the first one in the settlement. Everyone who could would come in to listen to the war news. One particular veteran of World War One could hardly be restrained from hitting the radio set when any news of a discouraging nature came in.

Chapter 21

Diary Excerpts 1940s

Excerpts from Myra's diary 1945-1949:

Wednesday, September 26, 1945: Very foggy, but wind has dropped at last. Delivered Diana finally with forceps at 7:35 a.m. Fine boy. Unable to rest so spend busy day only to be called 10:30 p.m. to M. H. who had a son at 11:35 p.m. Also a fine boy. *Northern Ranger* called a.m.

Monday, November 5, 1945: Rain and wind. Called 2 a.m. to Mrs. J. H. and delivered a son at 11:30 a.m. She was a splendid patient.

Thursday, November 8, 1945: Called at 11:30 last night to little S. G. who had a cold. Returned home to someone coming for me. Delivered O. H. a small baby boy 4:50 a.m. Nice cold dry night.

October 26, 1946: Usual busy day. Many patients as an epidemic of pink eye in here. Scare because diphtheria at Bonne Bay so I wired Department for particulars.

Thursday, October 10, 1946: Fine. Warmer. Trevor went back in woods again. Angus put out herring net. Took out 10 teeth for E. H., all she had.

Tuesday, October 5, 1948: Lovely warm smooth day. Trevor went off fishing and we had fresh cod for supper. Angus went up Parsons Pond with Alex so away for night. Did big wash.

Monday, March 22, 1948: Temperature up to 28 F. Lovely day. Bright and cold. Did big wash. Usual busy day. Angus hauling wood.

Wednesday January 19, 1949: Received first mail for winter which had been landed by plane at Port Saunders and brought up from there. Quite a big mail. Several patients during day including H. G. who had five upper extractions.

* * * *

Myra delivered her last baby at 11 p.m. on Christmas Day 1956. The baby boy was her grandson and he was named Noel. Myra's only son, Trevor, and his wife Mildred are Noel's parents. At the time of Noel's birth, they were living in Daniel's Harbour near Myra and Angus and Mildred had invited her in-laws to her house for Christmas Day dinner. Mildred had planned to go to the cottage hospital in Bonne Bay for the delivery of her youngest son, but when she went into premature labour on Christmas Day The Nurse and Angus immediately hurried to their house to get Myra's midwifery bag. The baby was safely delivered at home with no complications.

Chapter 22

The Life of a Working Mother

In serving the public very little consideration is given to the person who is thus compelled to trust her children in the tender mercies (or otherwise) of other people. This was forcibly brought home to me on many occasions.

For instance, my first child, daughter Grace, was entrusted to a relative at the age of one year. A few days later she nearly died with croup. I subsequently found that she had been prepared for bed at the correct time, but her sitter wanted to go visiting so with no more ado took the baby out into the frosty weather and to an over-heated house. Late at night, the baby was returned and put to bed in a cold house. No precautions were taken, such as wrapping the child to protect her from the cold.

A few years later I was detained to attend to a baby case and so permitted a relative to take Grace home by steamer. On the trip, she was exposed to another child who was suffering from whooping cough. Upon my return, I found Grace quite ill, and when I warned everyone concerned to avoid the house I was, of course, considered ridiculously over anxious about my child.

When, however, the infection spread, the scoffers were

quite ready to get me to attend to their children, regardless of my own child's need. Then, when the accident happened to my brother-in-law, Alex, it was necessary once again to leave the child, now 2-1/2 years old. This time, no physical accident happened to her, but she was so pampered and not corrected that I had to use stern measures upon my return. For the first three nights after my return, she clung to me, holding my face between her two hands and almost standing in my lap to maintain contact, even when sleeping. It took several days to overcome her fear of being left again.

My small son, at about one year of age, was left in the care of a girl who was acting as housemaid for me. During my absence, this girl had removed a very hot damper from the wood burning stove and laid it on the floor on a sheet of tin, away from the stove and in the path of anyone coming near to it. Needless to say, a small child stumbling around a kitchen just had to be the victim. Trevor fell with two hands coming into contact with the hot damper. Again, upon my return, I had a sick child to be anxious about. He bears the scars to this day, nearly 40 years later.

On another occasion he was struck insensible by another child, who hit him with a frozen junk of wood, striking him on the cheekbone under an eye. Grace ran in saying he was lying on the snow and would not get up. Poor lad. How could he? He was insensible. I got him in and spent a very anxious night with him. I would have given an arm to have had a doctor or hospital to take him to.

The youngest child, Barbara, fared almost as badly. One evening, returning from a full day of cases and sitting to supper with Barbara in her chair, I remarked that she seemed listless. "Well," said the girl who had been in charge of the house, "she did hit her head today. We were running around playing when she fell and struck her forehead right across the edge of an open drawer." No sooner had I heard this than

Barbara began to twitch and commenced convulsions. We took her and put her in a warm bed and observed her carefully for the next 24 hours. Fortunately, there was no recurrence and Barbara recovered with no after effects.

But even when the children had grown up and could look after themselves there seemed to be things happening which might not have happened if I had them under my own care continually.

On one particularly bad occasion, my son, now 19, became ill with a severe tonsillitis. At the same time, there was a badly hemorrhaging woman in a camp some miles away, and another woman nearer, who suffered with TB plus pregnancy, plus toxemia, plus the severest constipation I ever knew. What followed was nightmarish, between trying to put in all the time with a patient who was in a lumber camp and with trying to empty the woman who was so toxic and in between snatching a little time to try and get nourishment into my very sick son.

As soon as it could be arranged, I prepared to move the patients to hospital. It was January, we had no road nor bridge over the intervening ponds and river, and the marshes were not solid enough to take any weight across. However, the hemorrhaging patient could now be left, so we set off with two sleds with one patient on each. Sadly, the pregnant toxic woman died en route. Trevor spent a month in hospital and then came home where he spent another month under my care. I am happy to say he made a complete recovery.

* * * *

Life was so different when I first came to Newfoundland that today it seems like another country altogether. The coming of Confederation made all the difference. Family allowances helped with education, clothing and medical services for families. In Daniel's Harbour, which is no longer isolated, we have young people able to remain at school and eventually proceed for higher education and professional life. Quite a number of our girls have become trained nurses with an RN certificate, lads have become teachers, some have acquired a B.A. Others have attended trade school and become proficient at their chosen jobs.

But none of this prosperity has altered the basic gentleness of the Newfoundlanders as I found them. He, and she, still 'go the other mile' when needed.

So, after 45 years here, can it be wondered that I stay and love the country?

After the war-torn years in England: air raids, relatives in the trenches, the heavy load of work because of the 'call up' of doctors, the increases of births due to shifting populations coming into my area for war work, of rationing, of little food and of finally finishing up with the dreadful influenza epidemic ... after leaving all of that behind and exchanging it for clean wholesome surroundings, an abundance of fish in the ocean and deer, moose and rabbits on the land, and with berries for the picking and fuel for the gathering, is it any wonder that to me Newfoundland was Utopia?

If I had to, I would do it all over again!

Epilogue

Myra practiced preventive medicine, did a lot of teaching and used plenty of common sense. She was a great improviser, using beach rocks as weights for broken limbs and cozily lined shoe boxes as incubators for babies. She found that much of the nutritional value of food was lost as people tended to overcook meat and vegetables. She encouraged the women to make a mild spruce beer, with minimal alcohol content, to stimulate appetite. She slowly and surely got the message across that while TB was the most serious problem and was contagious, the next most serious problem was a matter of education as to cooking and the proper foods to eat.

After Myra's first few years in Daniel's Harbour, the Committee which had sponsored and financed the introduction of the first nurses to Newfoundland, NONA, merged into a larger association, NONIA (Newfoundland Outport Nursing and Industrial Association). Founded in 1920, and incorporated as a non-profit business in 1924, the purpose of the association was to assist Newfoundland outport communities to access health services by raising money from the sale of hand-knit garments to pay the salaries of public health nurses.

When Myra's NONA contract expired, no nurse was sent to replace her. Instead, when NONIA was established, a nursing station was built at Port Saunders, located 30 miles to the north of Daniel's Harbour and a NONIA nurse put in charge there. Myra, however, continued to work as a volunteer because local patients demanded her service. She saw patients in her home for 10 years without the authority to recommend a patient to a hospital or dispense drugs.

In 1934, she was placed on the payroll (part-time) of the Commission of Government's Department of Public Health and Welfare. While she was in the employ of the Department, earning $250 a year, Myra was called upon to provide a six-month midwifery course to train a few local women of her choice. Throughout these years, she worked closely, through correspondence, with doctors in cottage hospitals in Norris Point, Bonne Bay, St. Anthony, and Port Saunders.

* * * *

Myra's life of service in her community included much more than just ministering to people's heath and welfare. She was also a woman of great faith who became actively involved in the church, playing the organ, organizing and singing in the choir, sewing surplices, teaching Sunday school and contributing to the church guild. She taught music at home, did sewing for people, and wrote letters for those who couldn't write or needed references. She was also a tireless advocate for improvements in her district.

Myra officially retired in 1953, but continued to see patients in her home until she was well into her 90s. In 1982, at age 92, she noted in her journal that she had carried out one tooth extraction for a boy of 14. She was active in the community, raising money for the building of a dispensary in 1954 and doing the book-keeping for her husband's store in Daniel's Harbour. She upgraded her accounting skills with a correspondence course in 1956. Myra started writing her memoirs in the 1960s.

Myra received several honours and distinctions for her work. In 1935, she received the King George V Jubilee Medal; in 1946 she was invested as a Member of the British Empire (M.B.E). In 1937, she received the King George VI Coronation Medal and in 1953 the Queen Elizabeth II Coronation Medal. In 1967 she became an honourary member of the Association for Registered Nurses of Newfoundland and Labrador (ARNNL). She became a member of the Order of Canada in 1974, the same year Memorial University bestowed upon her a Doctor of Science, Honoris Causa.

* * * *

Myra and Angus's children lived and thrived. Their two daughters became nurses, graduating from the St. John's General School of Nursing. Grace married, had four sons, and lives in Alberta. Barbara married, had two sons, and lives in Wawa, Ontario. Trevor is a retired businessman/politician who lives in Steady Brook, on Newfoundland and Labrador's west coast. He and his wife Mildred are the parents of five children, three sons and two daughters.

* * * *

Angus died on May 6,1993 at age 96. Myra was 100 when she died in Wawa, Ontario, on April 26, 1990. She and Angus are both buried in Daniel's Harbour Cemetery. Their house in Daniel's Harbour, including a clinic Angus added on for Myra in 1942, is now a restored heritage site and a museum dedicated to the outport nursing profession.

* * * *

Myra Bennett's life is the subject of Theatre Newfoundland Labrador's production of "Tempting Providence," a play by Robert Chafe which had its world premiere at the Gros Morne Theatre Festival in 2002 and has since toured nationally and internationally. Myra has been featured in articles in Weekend Magazine and Reader's Digest, in the book "Don't Have Your Baby in the Dory!" and in a CBC-TV documentary "Lady of the Lonely Places." Stories from her nursing career were portrayed in historical illustrations by Joan Horwood in 1975.

Bennett house